DOCTOR OF THE HEART

Doctor
of the
Heart

CONRAD W. BAARS, MD

Fr. George d. Gage
Ex weis livnis
1997

ALBA·HOUSE   NEW·YORK

SOCIETY OF ST. PAUL, 2187 VICTORY BLVD., STATEN ISLAND, NEW YORK 10314

Library of Congress Cataloging-in-Publication Data

Baars, Conrad W.
   Doctor of the heart : an autobiography / Conrad W. Baars.
       p.   cm.
    ISBN 0-8189-0717-7
    1. Baars, Conrad W. 2. Catholics — United States — Biography.
3. Psychiatrists — United States — Biography. 4. World War,
1939-1945 — Personal narratives, Dutch. 5. World War, 1939-1945 —
Underground movements — Netherlands. 6. Buchenwald (Germany:
Concentration camp) I. Title.
BX4705.B10155A3   1996
150'.92 — dc20   95-25824
[B]   CIP

Produced and designed in the United States of America by the
Fathers and Brothers of the Society of St. Paul,
2187 Victory Boulevard, Staten Island, New York 10314,
as part of their communications apostolate.

ISBN: 0-8189-0717-7

Printing Information:

Current Printing - first digit	1	2	3	4	5	6	7	8	9	10

Year of Current Printing - first year shown

1996	1997	1998	1999	2000	2001

How beautiful on the mountains are
the feet of the man who brings tidings of peace,
joy, and salvation. (Is 52:7)

Entrance Antiphon,
Feast of St. Luke, October 18

Preface

"It's a funny thing about life, if you refuse to accept anything but the best you very often get it." *W. Somerset Maugham*

The death of Dr. Conrad W. Baars reminds me that the road of mediocrity is the lot of most men. For Conrad Baars, the word which best describes his path is *excellence* — all the way.

His life was forged on the anvil of *Faith* and *Cross*. From his native land of the Netherlands through the death camp of Buchenwald, to his final resting place at Fort Sam Houston National Cemetery, San Antonio, Texas, Koert lived by experience the power of the Cross, the meaning of the Resurrection. Through *affirmation* he literally touched the lives of countless people. Priests and religious leaders throughout the world owe much to Dr. Baars. He had a special insight into their lives and problems; he was for us a *brother-Christ*. He taught us to share our humanity and to express our emotional life in a most positive manner. His profound respect for the priesthood of Jesus Christ and the life of dedicated service to the Lord in religious life made him most apt to reach out to the suffering and often times brought healing into their lives.

Dr. Baars was not blinded by the humanity of the Church. He was able like Christ to accept this and transcend to a higher realm. He valued the virtue of obedience as few of his contemporaries were able to do. In 1965 he wrote on the subject in *Cross & Crown*: "Obedience is indisputably one of the cardinal principles of medieval Western Christian society. It was indisputably thrown over when our secular modern Western society broke out of its religious chrysalis, and indisputably this modern society is now

vii

in grave difficulty... The word obedience is derived from the Latin words *ob* and *audire* and it means to listen to or to hear. The Dutch word, *gehoorzaamheid*, and the German word, *Gehorsam*, retain this same meaning. Through obedience, therefore, the subject hears and follows the voice of authority. ..." For Dr. Baars, the voice of authority was always the voice of Peter.

The day of October 22, 1981 was a rain-swept dreary day. Clergy, family and friends met at St. Luke's Catholic Church in San Antonio to bid farewell to a remarkable friend. Yet the spirit within the church was hardly somber. The Mass of Burial echoed the sentiments of Koert's life: love, hope and peace. At the end of the service, Msgr. Thomas J. Collins read from a favorite passage of Dr. Baars found in a book entitled: *He and I* by Gabrielle Bossis. In one of her conversations with Our Lord, she describes Him as saying: "When the moment of death comes for my friends, you believe, don't you, that I come gently, with all the delicate touches that you know, to take their souls into My Kingdom? You would do the same if you were taking someone into one of your beautiful homes. You would want to feel the joy of their surprise, wouldn't you? Then I, God, Who love more and own more, how could I fail to be interested in the passing of My friends from time? Nothing that you may possibly have imagined of the love of My heart comes anywhere near the reality. Remember that I wanted your joy so much that I came down to earth to know suffering. And when I see you suffer, and suffer for me, I gather each of your sufferings with great love, as though yours were greater than Mine, and had a value that My heart would like to make infinite. And this is why, when you allow me to do so, I merge your life with Mine."

Father John Powell, S.J., reminds us that there is an old Christian tradition that God sends each person into this world with a special message to deliver, with a special song to sing for others, with a special act of love to bestow. No one else can speak this message, or sing this song, or offer this specific act of love. According to this venerable tradition, "the message may be spoken, the song sung, the act of love delivered only to a few, or to all the people in a small town, or to all the people in a large city, or even to all the people in the whole world. It all depends on God's unique plan for each unique person. So from my heart I want to say this to you: 'Please believe that you have an important message to deliver, you have a beautiful song to sing, and a unique act of love to warm this world and to brighten its darkness.' And when the final history of this world is written, your message, your song, and your love will be recorded gratefully and forever."

This is what Dr. Baars meant by affirmation. Every man and woman is unique. A fitting epitaph for Koert might be this old Latin saying:

"Homo sum, humanum nihil a me alienum puto!" ("I am a man, and nothing human is foreign to me.") For Dr. Conrad W. Baars, *the best is yet to come!*

> Very Rev. Robert Silverman, VF
> Church of the Good Shepherd
> Schertz, Texas

Introduction

This book is dedicated to those whose suggestions immensely improved the smoothness of the manuscript: Mary Rosera Joyce, whose suggestions upon reading the raw manuscript made it read so much better; Nancy Hagen, whose editing was terrific, and Father Robert Silverman, whose persistence in getting us going to finish the manuscript and a publisher to read it paid off. Also Father William Virtue of the Peoria, Illinois Diocese, who suggested the title *Doctor of the Heart*, and who has always been a supportive friend.

And of course Michael Baars, who got me to type and correct the manuscript so well on the computer, and Sue, who worked very hard on it. I could not have done it without them.

The whole work is a labor of love in memory of a remarkable man of vision, the husband and father of our family. Conrad W. (Koert) Baars not only survived the horrors of a concentration camp, but he disseminated the remarkable ideas of Anna Terruwe, M.D., a Catholic psychiatrist from the Netherlands, blending the psychology of St. Thomas Aquinas with the authentic ideas of modern psychology. Uncounted people have been immensely helped, and are still being helped by the writings Koert left behind. Our hope is that more and more people and professionals will become acquainted with this work.

> The family of Conrad W. Baars
> Mary Jean Baars (Mrs. Conrad W. Baars)

PART ONE

≱ *I* ≰

In the years following World War I, my native land, the Netherlands, having just emerged from its successfully neutral position, enjoyed a stable government and an increasing prosperity, due to its trade with Germany and England, in addition to that of the Dutch East Indies. Sharing a common border naturally necessitated friendliness between Germany and the Netherlands, and it was this trade with its neighbors that was the foundation of the Dutch economy. Since most European nations possessed a limited capacity for production, friendly relations between countries were always desirable, which was especially true in the case of the Netherlands, and my tiny country produced an admirable prosperity under the reign of Queen Wilhelmina.

It was during this era of abundance that I was born in Rotterdam on January 2, 1919, the second son of affluent parents. My father, Walter Baars, a young attorney, was already beginning to see his own growing influence in the city. His ability to practice law was becoming known even beyond the limits of Rotterdam; he sometimes had the occasion to travel to Mexico on business. Father's family was originally from Hoofdplaat, a small village in the southern part of the country. Family life was shared with his parents and a sister who later entered the convent. It may have been during those important years that my father acquired a taste for books, then for law in particular. In any event, the limited surrounding of the Dutch countryside prompted his exodus to Rotterdam.

My mother was the former Constance de Groot, a lovely woman of medium height, with fair skin and blonde hair worn in the fashion of the day. She had come from a Rotterdam family of six girls and two boys, and had enjoyed the closeness of the large family. From this close-knit environment had been fostered her engaging manner and an interest in everything about her, which she passed on to all of us, her children.

As the family grew to encompass six children, my father's law practice also expanded as he became better known for his professional talent. It was his profession that often called him away from Rotterdam for increasingly longer absences, and which made his presence all the more precious to his children and wife when he returned. Yet, no matter how devoted we were to our parents, we, like our confreres, were subject to the vagaries of life in a post-Victorian household. As youngsters we were taken care of by a nurse, and it was only when we were old enough (around 12 or 13) to appreciate the merits of table manners that we were allowed to eat with our parents during the family meal. Despite the seeming austerity of this custom, however, we felt the affection of both our parents, who wholeheartedly loved us. Indeed, there were always those nights during the thirties when the dining room of the house on the Oudedijk rang with hilarity at the stories, jokes and puzzles which were the delight of all of us. The traditions of the Victorian world which surrounded us were simply understood to permit the lady of the house liberty to pursue her other "duties." Later, when the nurse left the household, Mother took over duties from which the customs of the era kept her, and lovingly attended her brood by herself.

Of all the children, I was Mother's favorite, not just in my opinion, but that of my brothers and sisters! Mother saw that I had inherited the determination of my father and her good humor. At least, that was what I understood her to think! Physically, my looks often recalled to mind my parents, possessing as I did the blonde hair and hazel eyes of my mother, and the firm jaw of my father, which often reflected the same characteristic stubbornness of my progenitors. Unfortunately, I had also inherited a receding hairline from Father, for even as a young man of 18, my hair (along with that of my brothers) began to thin out ever so steadily, though I never got as radically bald as my two brothers! Fully grown, my height matched my father's at 5'9" — I usually preferred to claim an extra inch — and my figure outfitted in a tuxedo, for the many parties my parents gave and attended, made a good impression.

An ardent desire for knowledge was something I was always aware of, a determination to try things, even if scary. Later in life I believed in the motto: "Live dangerously!" I certainly got the chance! I also had a sense of humor, even though I probably drove people crazy with my puns. There was one escapade that particularly stood out in my mother's mind when she remembered my youth. The house in which we lived was quite large, and even with several servants to help her keep an eye on her brood, mother did not always know what her pranksters were up to. In her gentle but firm way, she established order about the house, but because the first floor dining room, parlor and kitchen were off-limits for play, the second and third floor bedrooms often became the sites of an outpouring of imagination by my brother Walter Jr. and me. The event that became something of a family legend occurred when we were at that age where we delighted engaging in mischief of whatever form. Having eluded the younger children, who idolized us and so followed us everywhere, the two of us settled ourselves in a room on the third floor and set about discovering the wonderful qualities of fire: its soft glow and warmth, and its magical ability to "eat" paper, leaving only those marvelous blackened shreds floating into the air. It was simple enough for us budding scientists to contain our experiments in the empty hearth until, as one of us explained later, one particularly hot piece landed innocently in the full wastepaper basket! By this time Mother had been alerted — possibly through motherly intuition alone — to the presence of fire on the upper floors, and we could hear her ascending the stairs. At the doorway she quickly took stock of the situation, swept up the offending basket, and smartly disposed of it out the third floor window, from where it fell to the pavement below and harmlessly spent itself. As I recalled it later, the incident occurred the very same day that I received my First Holy Communion!

Mentioning my First Communion brings up the fact that we

were a Catholic family. Holland at that time was one-third Catholic and two-thirds Protestant. Socially, those of us with different religions did not associate with each other. As Catholics there were many of us who entered religious orders or who became missionaries. The strong faith I inherited was to be life saving for me in the future when I faced the Nazi menace.

Other things I remember are the games which children were apt to play. One such pastime was the ever-popular telling of scary stories in a darkened room. Walter Jr. was favored to tell the story, but my role was to seek out a "victim" and, at precisely the most chilling moment, grab his or her ankle. The screams and giggles which broke the darkness were a delight to me as well as to my brothers and sisters, and so a rainy day — and there are many of them in our northern country — was usually taken up with such satisfying occupations.

My learning to react quickly to circumstances as well as my sense of humor developed in youth would years later not only save me time and again from the Nazis, but would preserve my sanity, once within the confines of the terrible Buchenwald concentration camp. Nevertheless, despite my evident enjoyment of the mischief to which my brothers and sisters were often subject, I was a quiet boy on the whole, and with adolescence came an ardor for study which virtually compelled me to devour books in my bedroom retreat. I also loved sports and played soccer, tennis and often went horseback riding. Bicycling in Holland and its bordering countries, Belgium and Germany, was naturally "de rigueur," because of the flatness of the lands and the proximity of cities; consequently, one summer saw me as a 16-year-old and several friends on a trip through Germany. As young Dutchmen, we expected no problem with the German language since it was so closely related to our own, and the gymnasium (or high school) had prepared us well in it. After the war, though, I found it almost impossible to speak in that language again. Like their fellow Europeans, the Dutch schooled their children thoroughly in the liberal arts — including French, English, Latin and classical Greek, history, civics, science and mathematics — with rewarding results. So, as young Dutchmen, we were confident and knowledge-able as we crossed into Germany on a sightseeing tour in 1935.

All of us had been to Germany before with our families, usually to vacation at the spas there. Those occasions heretofore had always been happy ones for me, filled with fun and leisurely strolls on the arms of my mother and father, eating German sausage specialties at the cafes of Bavaria, or in the quaint little towns we had frequented while in Germany. For me, this beau-tiful country had always recalled to mind the aroma of weiner schnitzel and days passed in cajolery and laughter. However, the Germany of the early thirties had seen the rise of the Nazis, and stories of their barbarism and corruption had reached the Neth-erlands and overseas. Reports of "extermination" of the insane and even those who were only physically indisposed came from hospitals. Nazi cruelty was known to prescribe castration, steril-ization and even forbid marriage to those considered unfit for propagation of the "Master" race. Inability to earn a living, along with degeneracy due to physical illness or feeblemindedness were cited to support such monstrosities. Under the guise of purification for the betterment of "humanity," individual men, women and children were suffering untold atrocities. While these reports were confined to sources such as hospitals and institutions — and, as such, boded no imminent threat to us as young travelers — my father was a cautious man and had realized the potential explosiveness of the situation in Germany and its consequences for the nearby Netherlands. Indeed, while others ignored or even refused to believe these reports, Father's foresight was unique, and early in the Nazi reign in Germany he had begun stocking imperishable provisions in the cellar of the large house. In the back yard a bomb shelter was constructed and stood as an ominous portent of things to come. Yet, even while Father had appraised the situation and prepared his family for the threat, and my comrades and I had been somewhat readied for the insidious changes which were taking place in Germany under the increasing influence of the National Socialist move-ment, led by Hitler since 1933, no one could have prepared us for the drastic transformation which it would forcibly make on our own lives in the years ahead.

During the rise of the National Socialist Party (NSDAP) in the twenties and early thirties, the first to be attracted by the speeches of the charismatic Hitler had been the farmers and the working class. Having literally risen to the top of the party within a few short years, Hitler drew others to himself almost magnetically. The First World War had left hundreds of thousands of Germans destitute and despairing, but the personal fascination of Adolf Hitler had given the victims of the postwar hyper-inflation new hope. Once the ostensible cause of their plight — the Jewish bankers and businessmen — was pinpointed by the dark-haired, mustachioed young Austrian, a light had been lit beneath them that was not to be easily quenched. It was the Jews, alien to their country, who had usurped their rightful places and who intended to dupe them into poverty and misery. A united Germany mandated the expulsion of the "anti-race" — that race which did not belong to any nation, but was only a parasitic nuisance to many. At the same time that this workers' movement gave voice to its anti-semitism, Hitler's suggestion of a pure German race was swept up with determination and fanaticism. Thus, fascination with the "Fuehrer" (as Hitler later demanded to be called) and his policies came largely out of the discontent of the lower working classes. By 1933, when Hitler had overthrown the Weimar Government, he had a large following which would obey him unwaveringly.

The outward transformation of Germany from republic to dictatorship was a subtle one, although manifestations of the change were occasionally visible to us as we rode through the country, in infrequent posters and swastikas. The threat, of which we were aware, did not disturb us, for neither we nor our countrymen suspected that only a few short years later we would see the pall of Nazism covering our own beloved homeland. I, like the rest of the Dutch, was comforted by the knowledge that, in the extreme case of war, the Netherlands would be able to remain neutral as it had in World War I.

❧ 2 ❧

1936 saw me at Oxford in England. My father realized the importance of knowing English well, for the Netherlands no longer possessed the influence it had in earlier centuries, and Dutch was a language which no one needed or desired to learn. English, on the other hand, was the new "international" language. It was a necessity for Dutchmen especially to acquire fluency in English — since no one would bother to learn Dutch — and Father encouraged its use at the dinner table by telling jokes in English. One such favorite of his was a puzzle which we all enjoyed, yet had to rethink upon each subsequent re-telling. Being a well-versed attorney, Father relished the logic required in this particular conundrum, and savored its delivery: "A man is looking at a portrait of a man. While he does so, he says, 'Brothers and sisters I have none, but this man's father is my father's son.' Who is the man in the painting?" Immediately six sets of vocal chords were engaged, ready with theories, explanations, and questions. The answer had been elucidated long ago, but we reveled in its rediscovery, for the answer alone was worth nothing if one did not understand the principle by which it was gotten.

I in particular enjoyed these intellectual calisthenics; they challenged me to stretch my understanding into a sort of logical spring, ready to silently leap out at anything which came to my attention. As in high school, I enjoyed my studies and worked diligently for a year at Oxford. Not only did my English improve through classroom hours and foreign friends, but it was here that I was first introduced to philosophy. At Campion Hall, I studied under philosophy professor Father Martin D'Arcy, the head of the department, a Jesuit who had authored several books on the relationship between divine and human love. I acquired a limited

9

philosophical background in my short year there, as well as a deep affection and regard for Fr. D'Arcy. It was to his works, among others, that I would someday look for guidance in my own psychiatric practice.

Less philosophical moments at Oxford were often spent with my two great Spanish friends, twins Joaquin and José Maria de Muller, from Barcelona. Naturally our fluency in English increased, since apart from French, it was the only language the three of us had in common. All three of us considered ourselves intelligent, and charmingly gallant as well, in the polished continental manner of the day, and these qualities, we felt, made us attractive to others. We were, on looking back, probably insufferable! We belonged to a group of young men and women studying at Oxford with whom we shared outings of horseback riding, tennis, and hours of exploration of the quaint English towns. My closeness to the twins solidified over the years, and during the war they would generously offer me refuge from the advancing German intruders.

The year at Oxford passed swiftly and 1937 saw me back in the Netherlands. The next two years I spent in study at the Dutch university of Delft, applying myself to chemical engineering. By 1939 I knew that my vocation was not in the sciences as such, but in a field through which I could personally help people: medicine. My uncle Marius van Boudijk-Bastiaanse, husband of my mother's sister Miep, was the ideal doctor to whom I looked for inspiration. My decision to enter the profession led me to the University of Amsterdam, where Uncle Marius was head of the Medical School. In the same year, with the mobilization of the Dutch armed forces in defensive preparation for war and Hitler's invasion of Poland, I joined the Royal Dutch Army. At the same time, feeling the cramped situation in the Netherlands and Europe infringing on me more and more, I added my name to a quota list of those who desired to emigrate to the United States. While the process sometimes took years, my intensely private personality so demanded the freedom which I believed only America had to offer that I was willing to wait. I dearly loved my family, but I elected to sacrifice the comfort of staying in my native land for what the hope of the United States promised.

During the wait to hear about emigration, I settled into studies at the medical school in Amsterdam. I lived with my dear aunt and uncle, Marius and Miep van Boudijk-Bastiaanse. Tante Miep was my mother's sister — a petite woman with an endearing smile whose sweetness drew me to her as to a second mother. My uncle Marius was a principled physician who had long ago won my admiration and love. In fact, it had been largely he who had influenced me to enter medicine. The couple was childless, and so welcomed the chance to open their home to me and my brother Walter, who was studying law in Amsterdam at the same time.

Despite the threat of war and the economic trouble which was the result of interrupted trade between the Netherlands and Germany, my life in Amsterdam was pleasant. I was studying medicine, which held a fascination for me. Yet my father's prediction of war with Germany was becoming increasingly real. Since the last months of 1939 and spring of 1940, the Dutch had begun to feel the effects of the war between Germany and the Allies: the British blockade prevented our usual trade with Germany, and it became difficult to continue as before without the raw materials obtained from there. Besides this, Dutch merchant ships were being sunk in the English Channel. We wanted to do just as we had in the war of 1914 — remain neutral — but at last the German invasion on May 10, 1940, the bombing of Rotterdam four days later, and subsequent capitulation to the intruder, changed our stance into one of great anger and resentment, and our quiet nation became a country of stubborn resistors.

With the bombing of Rotterdam, Germany revealed its iron-fisted intentions: the Reich had broken the Geneva Convention under which treaty warring parties were not to attack undefended cities. Hitler was incontestably unscrupulous, a man under whom Europeans would never be free; from the first, his tactics were devious, purporting to be the "protector" of the countries he had invaded. The May 14th bombing of Rotterdam decimated the heart of the city, killing 900 and leaving thousands homeless. Residential areas were also affected. Our house on the Oudedijk was no exception, with one bomb falling directly on the kitchen, but fortunately father's diligent precautions saved the family: the bomb shelter in back of the house shielded them from the effects of the barrage.

The German violation of Dutch neutrality was obviously unacceptable. Hitler's excuse was that Germany needed strategic air bases in the small country in order to arrange the coming attack on England. By invading, Hitler asserted, Germany was merely putting the Netherlands under the "custody" of the German High Command in order to preserve its neutrality from the Allies. In actuality, Hitler's aim was to eventually annex the Netherlands for the purpose of furthering the "Aryan race" with pure Teutonic stock — Dutch blood. What Hitler and his henchmen did not expect to encounter was the Dutchman's pride. Through five hard winters Dutch stubbornness would prevail over German ruthlessness and, even with the aid of 100,000 Dutch Nazis, the spirit of the Netherlands would not be broken. Although in only five days the Netherlands went from being a free and prosperous nation to subjugation of the worst kind, the oppression with which the Germans expected to crush Dutch resistance only served to further unify Dutchmen in a common purpose: to defeat the oppressor.

The first days of Nazi domination were dazed for us. Shock and disbelief paralyzed everyone. In the beginning of the occupation life seemed to retain its normalcy, as the Germans attempted to mask their true intentions in order to make domination all the easier for themselves. They alleged that they were Holland's protectors from Allied invasion! However, the insidiousness of their presence soon became apparent as freedoms were curtailed, and more and more German-appointed Dutch Nazis were given free rein. Friction between them and the public increased as the formerly-incarcerated traitors forced their propaganda upon the population, evincing their anti-Semitism and atheism. Despite oppression, the Dutch on the whole possessed two inherent traits that aided them in their resistance: strong family ties and religious beliefs. As such, the Dutch were firmly bound by values that had been passed down for ages. While practicing religious toleration, the Dutch maintained their fidelity to the Judeo-Christian tradition and it was this belief, along with a natural stubbornness, that cemented our lives. Indeed, while being one of the smallest countries had made us particularly vulnerable to just such an attack, we had long before developed our internal resources of faith and patriotism, and it was these characteristics that would bring us through the pitiless years of occupation. As a Dutchman, I had my share of these qualities, borne out in my resilience to the suffering which I would experience. I was to know quickly what the Germans intended.

❧ 3 ❧

"A shave? No, I just shaved at home." I looked around the shop unbelievingly. How was I here? I sat dazed in my wonderment.

The barber waited patiently, then said quietly, "You don't need a haircut either; as you know, you were here two days ago."

Then I realized what had happened and was irritated at myself for having lost this time when I had an appointment to keep. I had been on my way on the streetcar to catch the 10:15 train to Rotterdam. Then suddenly, with no recollection of how I got there, I found myself sitting in the barber chair. Evidently I had gotten off the car with the crowd at the Leidschestraat and walked in a trance to the barber's.

Now that I had come to my senses, I got up quickly and ran out of the shop. I caught another streetcar headed for the station, but I was already late. My train had gone, so I had to wait thirty minutes for the next one. I paced the platform trying to figure out my strange actions.

Finally on the train, I was able to relax, but when we stopped at Leiden for the five minutes that grew into twenty, I knew something was happening. The rest of the passengers had become as restless as I had, sitting there waiting. Conversation became general, the rumors more fantastic as to the reason for our delay. In Holland in November 1942 after the Nazi bombing, invasion and persecutions, there were always rumors.

We soon found out that the train ahead, the one I would have been on if I had not wandered aimlessly into the barbershop, had been machine gunned by Allied fighter planes. The wreckage was horrible, cars had overturned with the sudden stop, and the whole train was burning and wrapped in flames. Above it all rose the screams of the trapped and wounded.

The rest of the morning, I helped with the victims who were brought to the Leidenstation for aid. The sight of those wounded, riddled with bullets and some with arms and legs shot off, kept me saying prayers — thanking God that I had not been one of them.

Early that sunny Saturday morning, I had started out from Amsterdam where I attended medical school and met regularly with the "Illegality," to go to Rotterdam for an important appointment. In the streets, the hated German Police in their green uniforms paraded underneath the large posters which said, "The German Police, the Friend of the Children."

I had become used to them these last months — used to the sight of them, but never used to the satanic system of which they were part. My life was comparatively quiet and easy under the German occupation. I had not experienced any personal danger, as I was a student and so far the students had been left alone. This was an effective Nazi plan, for never was the Dutch population to be aroused at one time by rebellion against their measures. Each group was attacked separately and at intervals, giving the other groups a false sense of security. Physicians, lawyers, businessmen, Jews, Catholics — every kind of group was attacked in their turn, giving the others the illusion that they were safe for the time being.

And time was precious. Any day help might come to us who were so anxious to see the day of Germany's defeat and of Holland's freedom. And every man wanted to come through this hell with his family alive and his own property intact and out of the hands of the German "protectors."

This waiting and watching did not mean that the Dutch people were cowards; on the contrary, many heroic deeds were performed to save a life and to help one's neighbor in danger and difficulty. But these deeds were done "underground."

Openly, general rebellion was not only dangerous but hardly possible to organize. The stakes were too high; when a relatively small group like the Jews or the physicians was persecuted, the rest of the population was not expected to take an open stand against its persecutors, as then all of them would have undergone the same fate at once.

The Germans used the same procedure in amassing their loot. Had they taken all at once the things that they gradually confiscated during the five years of occupation, a serious revolt would have stopped them early in the game. When they took all of the copperware that had not been buried in the backyard or dumped in the rivers, people grumbled, but it was not such a serious loss that they would risk their lives in open revolt. It was the same when the Nazis came for the gold coins, the radios, the bicycles, the cars, the dogs and so many other belongings. So the Germans still got what they wanted and avoided bloodshed in getting it — not that they loved us so dearly — but only because it might cost the lives of a few of their own men.

And we learned from them. We used the same tactics. We never did away with the whole German battalion at once. We eliminated a few Nazis here and shot a few collaborators there, and we removed a fair total without invoking too many reprisals at once.

Until now I had not experienced any personal persecution, but soon I was to be on my own, no longer connected with the ties that normally held a son to his parents, a student to his university, a soldier to his regiment, or a citizen to his country. I was to be an outlaw fighting my own fight — to live and then to be free of Nazi slavery. And as I look back on that day late in 1942, when I was so inexplicably prevented from taking that ill-fated train, I can only be grateful that I was unaware of what the remaining days and weeks and months and years of World War II held in store for me.

≥ 4 ≤

The knock on the door was sudden and terrifying in the silence. I tried to press even closer to the cold stone wall in the darkness.

"Come out, come out, they have all gone," someone shouted on the outside.

Not one of the six of us moved or spoke. We were held in the spell of the quiet in the little room. Here we had hidden for two and a half hours. In the lower regions of one of the laboratory buildings of the University of Amsterdam we had waited for the German Police to find us.

The knock came again, and the voice said, "It's safe to come out. It's I, the janitor."

The building had been quiet for some time, so we felt safe in leaving our hideout. At least safe from immediate danger, for from this moment on, my life would not be safe until the door to freedom was opened more than two years later by the United States Third Army under General George Patton. That door was the gate to the Buchenwald concentration camp.

I had just escaped being taken prisoner in this raid on the University. All Holland was prisoner under the Nazis, but we students had been allowed to continue our education until the enemy decided to put a stop to it.

The realization that the time had come was in early December, 1942, when the Germans issued orders that all Jewish professors were to be removed from the university. This order aroused in the students the latent rebellion of many months. We were ready to act — to protest against this unfair discrimination. It did not take an organized meeting to move us to strike. But the dean, knowing our obvious feelings and intentions, stopped our action by making our Christmas holidays immediate.

Our reaction had been calculated by the Germans who seemed to be able to judge accurately the result of most of their orders. They knew of our intention to strike, and they knew it had been avoided only by the sudden vacation. It was their move now. They told us that we must return to our studies under penalty of reprisal after Christmas. We knew that the Germans were not eager to have us complete our education. It had been clear that they greatly resented our continuing thorough studies while their Nazi students rushed through a shortened course in preparation for Hitler's army. We had been allowed to go on with our work as long as the time had not come for the Germans to stop it.

That time had come — not on the first day after the holidays when classes opened with only a few students — but six days later when the majority had returned after seeing the safety of those first few. How cunning were the Nazi plans. They could take us when they chose!

I was late that last morning for school, for I had to go on the slow, jammed streetcar to the eastern part of the city where my classes were being held. The University buildings in Amsterdam are not grouped together on one campus, but they are spread out over different parts of the city. When I got to the classroom in the laboratory building, I was lucky to find an empty seat in the front row. There I had the best spot to hear, and a chance to leave during the few minutes interval between lectures to smoke in the hall. The ones who sat in the back of the large classroom seldom took the trouble to leave for such a short time. I was soon to find out how lucky I had been to find that seat — it was to mean the difference between freedom and prison!

After the first lecture, I went into the hall to enjoy one of my hard-to-get cigarettes. Suddenly three students ran past me shouting: "The Germans! The Germans!"

I heard the sound of breaking glass and of running feet, both noises suddenly mixed into an uproar. I ran past the door of the classroom — the passage through which was blocked by a mass of pushing, fighting, and panicky students — and came to the steps that led to the basement.

It seemed as though I was watching myself as I methodically explored the basement for an escape. I had waited a long time until I myself would be the target for the Nazis. I had known that it would be soon, for the Germans were concentrating on all Dutch students. Yet I did not fully realize the danger. I walked to the other side of the basement, where a few steps up was the back door. It seemed an escape. Climbing the steps softly, I came to an abrupt stop about four feet from a Nazi uniform and a Nazi machine gun!

The gun was pointed at me. This was real, and I felt real, especially as my heart beat relentlessly and endlessly in my chest. The gun was aimed at me, but the man behind the gun had his back to me. He was enjoying the chase and the capture of the students on the first floor. My impulse was to leap on him and take over the gun. But it would not have helped us for long, because there were always more Nazis and more guns. I backed slowly down the steps into the enfolding shadows of the lower floor.

This brief episode left me with a frantic desire to hide, for that was my only chance against this enemy. It seemed impossible to find a place that the Germans, in their plodding but thorough way, would not discover.

"I must be quick now," I thought. The sounds were more violent than ever. Even as I listened, noises began on the staircase from which I had come. I ran into a dark, short hall.

"Here's a door, open it fast, get inside, behind those charts," I was ordering myself.

I had started to get behind storage racks, containing life-sized anatomical drawings, when the door of the small room opened. Before I had time to think, five students rushed in and found themselves placed with me behind the charts.

It was silent then in our hideout, but the pursuit went on above us. Finally, we could no longer hear the shouted orders of the German Police, nor their pounding heavy boots. It would not be long before the basement would be searched. Even at that thought came the sounds of footsteps which hesitated in front of our door. That minute... while we waited for the decision of the searcher outside… was interminably long. It was a time for solemn prayer.

"Dear God, keep us safe," I kept forming on my lips. We heard the footsteps grow softer until they died away.

Two and a half hours we waited in that dark, musty place. But I was almost content to stay in its safety, for I knew when I stepped out, I would begin a life of uncertainty and constant apprehension. I cursed myself for having walked into that Nazi trap by returning to school.

Every minute that we waited, pressed against that stone cold wall, our hope of escape grew. It had been silent in the building for a long time, when suddenly the whole building began to vibrate under heavy footsteps. Motors outside started to run, then again silence — a deep, intense, frightening silence.

"The Germans must have left and taken all the students along," someone whispered. Still we did not dare to move. It was a short time after this that the janitor knocked on the door and called to us.

Back again in the classroom, we found a frightened group of girl students, who told us that the police had searched the building from top to bottom and had driven all the students together into the classroom where they were covered by machine guns. Several Nazi students had helped the Germans search the prisoners for arms and illegal papers. Then those boys were loaded into cars to go into the first well-known stop on the way to Germany — the concentration camp of Vught, in the south of the Netherlands.

Our little group in the basement, and a few others who had hidden on the second floor where the notice on the door "Danger — Pestroom" kept the Germans from going in, had escaped.

When I reached my rooms, I heard that raids had been made simultaneously on all University hospitals and classrooms and on the library, so that no one could have been warned.

The next day I left Amsterdam to start a new life of uncertainty, of being chased about, of escaping from numerous raids in trains and streets, of sleeping every night at another address with family and friends.

≈ 5 ≈

It should have been a warning when I saw the Dutch Nazi student staring at me as I got on the train to go home. I remembered him and how surprised he was when he saw me talking to the girls in the classroom after the raid. I did not think twice at the time of seeing him at the railroad station until two days later when the German police simultaneously raided my rooms in Amsterdam and my old home in Rotterdam. Fortunately I was not home that night as my brothers and I had thought it safer to disappear for a while. None of us was taken at that time, although the Dutch informer was on the job.

It occurred to me that I had better watch my steps more carefully, especially as I had received several letters of summons to go to Germany not long before. I had been working in small underground groups as secrecy in the larger Dutch underground was hardly possible in the long run. Too many of those belonging to the larger "official" illegal groups were arrested continually. Even so, my name was on the list of undesired persons which the occupier kept.

During the severe winter of 1941-1942 I had been one of the first persons to be forced to do sentry duty in front of "German buildings" in Amsterdam, as reprisal for a bomb that had exploded in one of the Dutch Nazi headquarters. It was far from pleasant to guard these buildings in the snow and ice when the temperature was fourteen below zero, though I never regretted being chosen for this honor.

At police headquarters, the muster place for all the "delinquents," one met interesting and important people. Each one had been chosen because of his known or suspected antipathies towards the Nazis and their Dutch collaborators. A strong band

21

of friendship developed between us during the nights and days that we did sentry duty. There followed get-togethers where professors, bank directors, businessmen, and students banded together to plan ways to thwart our enemy, and in a brotherly fashion we drank toasts to the destruction of the German Reich and the N.S.B., the National Socialist Movement in the Netherlands.

Perhaps there was something good in National Socialism, but nobody could ignore the way it pursued its goal: the horrifying means, the terror and the crimes that it did not hesitate to use as its tools. That was sufficient to cause me to despise this system and its makers in the depths of my heart, and to urge me to do my part, however small it would be, to jam a spoke in its wheels.

Until now I had given little thought to politics, and had felt content to dream of a Christian "Communism," based on the principle of treating your neighbor like yourself, as the ideal form of government. However, I now saw that I was wrong. I realized it was necessary to support actively that form of government which could and would give its proper place to this elementary Christian principle. Nazism, Fascism, and Communism as preached by Moscow were all based upon power and terror and were thus entirely inconsistent with the idea of a Christian Communism. I saw clearly that I had not only to oppose and fight these systems, but also to promote a democratic government, either in the form which had brought America its greatness as a constitutional republic, or under a constitutional monarch, of which the Netherlands could be called an excellent example.

For the first enterprise the time had arrived now, for the second one I would have to wait until the world knew peace again.

A few weeks after the raid on the University, my older brother, three other students from Rotterdam and I had been put on a special list by the Nazis, to undergo, in case of our refusal to obey the summons to go to Germany, special reprisals. We would be a deterrent example for others. I steamed open the envelope with the first summons I had received and found that I was ordered to go to Hamburg as a common laborer. Hamburg seemed an unhealthy place to me, as it was being bombed heavily by the Allies, so I returned the letter with the notice on the envelope "Addressee absent." In the weeks that followed, I received so many similar notes that I no longer took the trouble to return them.

The students now had time away from their studies to devote to sabotage. The Germans realized that something must be done, the more so as the execution of five students from Amsterdam, convicted for the dynamiting of several German trains, had not brought the desired effect. On the contrary, acts of sabotage became more numerous every day.

The occupier offered the students a chance to continue their studies on the condition that they sign a declaration of loyalty to the German occupation in Holland, that they promise to refrain from further hostile acts, and that they pledge themselves to go to Germany once they had completed their studies.

It was clear that signing such a promise would have been a crime not only against our own conscience but also against the Dutch people, who expected open resistance from the student group to a German order that was hostile to the general welfare.

Most of us refused to sign but there were some students who went along with the demand, and as always a few who were afraid to get into trouble. The refusal of the majority to return to school under the impossible conditions put down for us disrupted completely the university education.

Then on May 5th, 1943, the evening papers carried a summons that all students who had refused to sign the declaration of loyalty were to present themselves within the next twenty-four hours to various places in Holland, from where they would be sent to Germany. There, each of them would be assigned to work in his own special field — this to make the bait more palatable! If they did not comply with the order, reprisals would be taken against their families — reprisals ranging from confiscation of property to death.

So we had twenty-four hours in which to give ourselves

over to the Nazis. If we did not, our families would be in mortal danger. It was a hard choice, and the time was short. But for most of us, a minute, a second, just the time to say no should have been enough time in which to give our answer. We had pledged ourselves from the first as good Christians and loyal patriots never to voluntarily give up to the Nazis. I refused the first summons; I would refuse the last. The answer was simple for me. Not so for others — for a few thousand students did obey the summons, and without doubt they regretted it for what was left of their lives.

On this May 5th afternoon when I saw the summons, I knew that the time had come for me to leave Holland. My family would be endangered for my opposition to the German Command. My patriotic duty was clear to me. However, it was easier to know it than to carry it out.

As I had already begun plans to go to France with two friends, where we were to help people escape by other means than the direct but precarious route by boat from Holland to England, I had to think of some way to gain time to arrange my own escape. The thought of being on that train for Germany with thousands of students made me feel sick. That very feeling gave me a thought.

I would be sick! Yes, my right side was hurting; surely, my appendix must come out this very day. A little while later I was at the house of a friend and neighbor — a surgeon.

He greeted me with, "Good day, Koert, you are looking well."

"Good day, Doctor, that's what I came to see you about. Did you see in the papers the orders for the students to report?"

"Yes, I did," said my friend. "You are to report within twenty-four hours. I saw it."

"That's right — and I am making plans to go to France. What I need is time, and an appendectomy — yesterday."

"Yesterday?" the doctor stared at me.

"The operation must be recorded before the date of the appearance of the summons. Would you help me?"

"What do your parents think of this, Koert?"

"I have just talked it over with them, and they approve. So it's up to you." I waited for his answer.

He picked up the telephone. "This is Doctor Bast. I want to schedule an appendectomy for tomorrow morning at eight o'clock."

⤞ 6 ⤝

The train sped on to Paris, and I was on the train. I closed my eyes, and remembered the recent, sad good-byes to my family. My parents had helped me to be strong. They had stood behind me in my determination to escape the German oppression. And they had let me go with quiet hearts, thinking I was in the care of an expert underground worker who had made this trip to Paris many a time. Had they known that my next stop after Paris would be Cherbourg, one of the centers of German fortification on the Atlantic Wall, they would not have known another hour's peace of mind. They had given me their blessings, which was the best thing they could give in those days of little blessedness.

And so I had left to fight the Nazis in whatever way I could — alone and without identity. For safety purposes I would henceforth have to live under an assumed name.

The train was slowing down, and I opened my eyes and saw that the bright summer sun was gone. We were pulling into the station at the Dutch-Belgian border. When we stopped, all the passengers in my compartment got up to go through customs. I followed them out. This would be the test of my forged papers, according to which I was a laborer with a Dutch-Nazi contractor in Cherbourg, and I was reporting back to work after a short leave in Holland. The papers were those of Todt, a German organization with which Dutch, Belgian and French contractors built the fortifications on the West Wall.

These Todt papers when blank were extremely valuable to a fugitive. The owner having filled in the required answers was assured a safe journey with no questions asked. It had taken a long time to get these papers; my recent appendectomy had served its purpose well!

There had been some changes in my plans. Chris, or King Kong, about whom I shall tell more later, was to make the trip with me. As he was an expert in all phases of underground activities, I had lost all my qualms about the dangers connected with this trip. However, at the last moment he had been forced to let me go by myself. Also, he had entrusted to my care two young Dutch boys who were unable to speak German or French. For safety I had seated them together in another car, and I looked for them as I walked nonchalantly to customs. I was sure there would be no trouble.

A German officer was inspecting the passports and papers. After he had looked over mine, he told me to step inside and wait. The other passengers returned to the train. I waited. The familiar fear of being caught came back to me. I began to doubt the value of the papers, or perhaps the officer had realized that my hands were not those of a seasoned laborer. I thought a thousand thoughts as I stood there. My outward calm and self assurance was holding up, but my pulse was beating faster and faster.

Finally the officer came out of his cabin and said: "Come with me!"

We walked back along the station and came to the platform of the train where a German soldier was posted. Handing him my papers the officer spoke again, "Here is a German soldier."

I opened my mouth to protest, but before I could speak, the real German soldier handed my papers to me. It was all right. I could enter the train.

The two boys in my care had been wise and stayed in their seats as laborers for the Todt Organization, who like all good soldiers are above the mass of ordinary citizens. It was a little late for me to remember that we did not have to leave our seats for customs inspection. My mind had been full of instructions and my thoughts had been on the course I was to follow when we arrived in Paris. But now that we were on our way again I began to relax. In Paris I put the two boys on a train that would take them to Tours where they were able to get help to continue their journey to Spain.

The evening air was cool in Paris. I could not help thinking of the bygone days I had spent in this always amazing city. I leaned against a tree and gazed into the sky. The present came back with a shock, for as I was fingering the back of my coat lapel, I had touched something that was pinned there. It was a badge of the Netherlands Union, a semipolitical organization forbidden by the Nazis. I could not move for a moment. How could I have been so stupid as to leave it on my coat? Unpinning it, I turned and stuck the pin deep into the bark of the tree. If it had been discovered on me back there at the border, my days as a free man would have been over then and there.

Gay Paris, "the City of Lights," had changed unmistakably since my last visit there in the summer of 1939. I felt it more than I could see or hear it; there was something apart from the numerous German uniforms in the streets, apart from the serious faces of the civilians and the half empty cafes. There was something that told me that Paris was dead. It was like a prescription in which two incompatible elements are united to form a substance that makes the prescription worthless for its original intention. So it was with Paris; two incompatible people, two extremely different ideologies had been forced together. The result was death.

Paris can only be Paris when the Parisians are alive and full of spirit and full of youth. Paris filled with beings devoid of that precious sense of humor which gives the wine of Bordeaux its sparkle and devoid of that spirited philosophy which gives the wine from Burgundy its heavy sweetness, a Paris filled with Huns is not Paris.

It was the place but not the time for sentiment. Two days I spent in Paris to make new contacts. One of them was with a man who worked as a disc-jockey for Radio Paris, which had its offices located on the Champs Elysees. This contact proved to be most valuable. And later on he announced our assumed French names on some of the regular request programs and played the records that had been requested by us. This was a convenient way of conveying certain messages to our friends elsewhere.

The day before I left Paris I cabled my friends in Cherbourg that I would arrive so they would meet me at the station. The train to Cherbourg was crowded with people who were fleeing the heat and the hunger of the big city, seeking a few weeks of rest and the well-filled tables of the country.

The first couple of hours on the train I did not feel at ease. Sitting on my bag in the narrow corridors, I became aware of the fact that my mind was trying to play tricks on me. I imagined that the Frenchmen around me were looking at me and talking about me in a suspicious way. I continuously heard words like "Dutchman" and "Netherlands" being mentioned in their conversation. More than once I had to wipe the drops of perspiration from my forehead. Undoubtedly these were illusions of reference similar to those as seen in cases of paranoid schizophrenia, contributing to feelings of guilt.

When we reached the coastal area, I became more at ease as only a few passengers who had special permits to enter that protected zone remained on the train. But I felt best of all when I saw my two friends from Rotterdam at the Cherbourg station.

My trustworthy travel papers had to be destroyed immediately upon arrival. There I was in the heart of the Atlantic Wall with no papers of identification, real or forged! I could not have returned to Paris if I had wanted to, as leaving the coastal zone was even more difficult than entering it.

I was dependent on my two good friends who had arrived two weeks previously and who knew well by now the situation in Cherbourg. They had already made valuable contacts with reliable individuals. They worked and slept in the office of the Dutch-Nazi chief of the contractor bureau. His having left for Holland made it convenient for me to move in with my friends at the office, which was next door to the Gestapo!

The evening following my arrival in the coastal city my friends and I went to Tourlaville, a nearby village renowned for its lobster and wine, for dinner to celebrate our successful reunion. With us were, among others, two French girls who worked for the Germans and so were able to provide me with a ration card for food.

The restaurant in Tourlaville was crowded that night. Only a few German soldiers were there. The other people were civilians who showed openly their hostile attitude toward our group, especially after a few glasses of wine had made our conversation a bit noisy. The people at the table next to us began to make remarks:

"How can you enjoy yourselves, you Nazis!"

The French girls tried to defend us and to answer their rebukes "They hate the Germans as much as we do."

But the answer was a hard laugh, "You, too, are the same — you work for the Nazis and their brothers. We should throw you all out." We deliberated for a moment, then started to sing, of all songs, the song of the Red Army! Before long, the customers left little doubt as to where their sympathies lay; their hostile remarks became fewer as we continued our singing. Soon everyone present in the restaurant had joined in — everybody, that is, except the German soldiers who, throughout the performance, retained their composure and did not appear at all disturbed. At any rate our ruse was successful.

My friends told me of how a few days before my arrival they had sung the same song while visiting a canteen of German marines in Cherbourg! Amazingly enough, the marines had joined in, first reluctantly, but then at the top of their voices in this song of their hated enemies. Evidently they either had never heard the song before, which I think is more probable, or they were not as Nazi as they ought to have been. The menacing looks had changed to smiles. We were comrades!

Back at the Todt office I groggily spread my bed on the floor in one of my friends' rooms, when suddenly there was a knock on the door.

"Come in!" we shouted. Never in my life did I regain sobriety so quickly as I did upon seeing three members in full uniform of the German field police enter the room. "Why didn't you black out the room?" came the demand.

"We forgot to do that," Dolf, who was not yet in bed, answered for us.

"What are you?"

"Dutchmen."

"What are you doing here?"

"We work for the Todt Organization."

"Where are your papers?"

Dolf frantically searched through his belongings. Even though he actually possessed them, he was so excited that he could not put his hands on them. Finally he was asked his name and other information, and then they prepared to leave, informing us that this would not be the end of it.

Then one of them turned on me asking, "Why are you sleeping on the floor?" Presumably it was not becoming for a member of the Todt Organization to sleep so simply on the floor.

To appease him, I replied that I had just returned from leave and that somebody else had taken my bed during my absence. Also that I had already put in my application for a new one.

The black boots whirled, barely missing my nose, and clumped out of the room. A few days later, we received a fine for three hundred francs which we promptly presented to the office for remittance.

We ate in a canteen for the Todt Organization, where I was admitted by means of a stolen permit. But before the week was over we had been rebuked twice for not saying, "Heil Hitler," and for not stretching our right arms in the customary Nazi way. So as to avoid further conflict, we had our meals when the Germans had finished theirs.

The day that the chief of the contractor bureau was scheduled to return from his trip to Holland, we decided that it would be better for all of us if I left Cherbourg. I had no official position there and would, by staying, only endanger the position of my two friends who needed only a little longer to finish the preparations for our underground operations elsewhere in France.

I went into hiding in the little village of Besnesville, about an hour by train from Cherbourg. It turned out to be a real vacation.

My host was Father Ryst, the priest of the village, and I shared the hospitality of his house with a number of French orphans to whom he was a loving father.

When I was not engaged in eating a dinner the like of which no longer existed in Holland at that stage of the war, I helped to harvest the potatoes in the garden or carried water to the plants or, best of all, slumbered in the shadow of the apple trees. At other times, I accompanied his sister-in-law Mrs. Ryst and the children on long walks through the woods where we gathered mushrooms and flowers.

Mrs. Ryst was always in the best of spirits, especially when her husband, Father Ryst's brother, had recently returned from a prisoner of war camp in Germany. It was she who filled in my French identification card which her husband had so cleverly forged.

I avoided the village completely and only went to Father Ryst's church on weekdays, when the only attendants would be one or two old peasant women. Nevertheless, it had soon leaked out that there was a stranger in the village, but to those who inquired personally with the priest, he replied that I was his cousin from Holland. This was quite plausible as his mother was Dutch and the priest himself knew the Dutch language quite well.

Yet, the days passed by too slowly. The daily news broadcasts from the BBC kept me on edge and made me feel guilty for enjoying such peaceful days when I should be engaged in more useful activities. However, there was nothing to do but wait until Herman and Dolf would give the word that we could go to Paris.

When the word came and I had to say farewell to these hospitable people, Mrs. Ryst wept, and I, too, felt the meaning of the French saying "Partir, c'est mourir un peu." ("Parting is to die a little.") But it was better to "die a little" now than by a longer stay to enhance the dangers they had risked so courageously.

Besides, there was work to do.

When we got to Paris, we needed certain special identification papers. We asked the help of a Frenchman, "Monsieur Pierre," who Mr. Ryst in Cherbourg had told us was a master in forging papers. After having called Monsieur Pierre on the telephone and been given the password, he invited me to come over to his apartment in one of the suburbs of Paris. It was a somber, rainy night when I alighted from the Paris metro. It had been an uneventful trip from the south side of the city where we were making our headquarters in the apartment house of a French-Dutch family near the Porte d'Orleans. I shook off the thought of what might have happened if I had not been successful in dodging the police, who at my transfer station had been checking the papers of all the passengers and searching them for weapons. I had jumped back into the train just before the automatically operated doors closed and continued my trip to the nearest station, from where I walked above ground to the next metro station of my transfer.

I had only a small Belgian "Mauser" in my hip pocket, but that would have been enough to have me arrested and make me miss my appointment that night.

By the time I approached the place of my rendezvous, it had stopped raining. The dark, wet streets were deserted as far as I could see in the moonless, starless night. Somehow I did not feel very much at ease, not only because this neighborhood was completely strange to me, but also because I knew that Monsieur Pierre was pretty "hot." I opened the door to the house and asked the janitor if Monsieur Pierre was at home.

"Never heard of him," he replied, and he turned around to go back to his room. As I had double-checked to be sure that I was at the right address by walking all the way around the block, I called out to him, "One moment, my friend." He stopped and came back.

"It is 7:45," I said, and without further hesitation the janitor opened the door of the elevator for me and told me to go to the sixth floor. While I was on my way up, the janitor must have given a signal as Monsieur Pierre awaited me in the dimly lit hall.

I gave him the password "Cherbourg-Paris."

Then he let me into his apartment. After I had given him the greetings from our mutual friend in Cherbourg, we got down to business and I explained what papers I wanted. He promised that he would have them ready in a few days, and would send them to our place by messenger. Just as I was ready to leave, a bell in the room rang sharply three times.

Pierre jumped up and whispered, "The Gestapo!"

He rapidly thrust some papers from the table into his pocket, switched off the lights, and opened the door. The elevator was already coming up. We ran up a stepladder and climbed through a trap door onto the roof of the building. Pierre pulled up the ladder, and just when I so softly closed the trap door, I heard the elevator stop. We tiptoed to the edge of the roof.

"Jump to the next building! " Pierre whispered, and momentarily switched on his flashlight. As it was too dark to see the depth below me, I jumped without fear. Through a trap door in the other building we let ourselves down to the sixth floor and to my surprise Pierre opened the door of a room next to the elevator.

He put on a small moustache and a pair of dark-rimmed glasses, and, smiling, he showed me his emergency identification card. The bachelor M. Pierre was now the widower Monsieur George Lamaison, ten years older and living at this address. George laughed and said: "This little trick has worked before. Let us hope it will again."

I had left my German and Dutch identification cards at home with Dolf and Herman, so I gave my gun to Pierre, who hid it in the bedroom with some papers. Then we sat down at a small table. If the Gestapo visited this building, too, they would find J. George Lamaison playing cards with M. Charles Burnell — and if we were lucky we would get away with it. After about forty-five minutes a bell rang twice.

"There is the signal," Pierre said. "The search is over. Let us go back to my room."

When I returned home shortly after midnight from this successful mission, I found Dolf nervously walking up and down the floor.

"Herman's been picked up by the police!" he said, before I had a chance to ask what the trouble was. "He was taking the

American fliers to the boarding house. Something must be done right away." He told me that an Englishman who worked on the police force of the French Surete had sent him word that Herman was at the police station at the Rue X, and that one could expect him to be shipped off to prison in Fresnes the next morning. From there it would be practically impossible to escape.

I knew where to go in an emergency like this, so after having fortified ourselves with some black coffee and a couple of black-market cigarettes, we were on our way to the hotel of Madame Rouge on the Avenue des Ternes. Here we found a Frenchman who knew exactly what to do to get Herman freed. From a nearby garage he got a brand-new car of German make, a B.M.W., and drove us to an old building in the Montmartre district not far from the notorious Place Pigalle.

Our case was explained to and discussed by several other Frenchmen who displayed great ingenuity. They got out some German S.S. uniforms bedecked with a couple of medals and the distinguishing marks of a Captain. Two of the Frenchmen put them on while another fixed some very important-looking documents. These papers contained an order that the prisoner, Herman, had to be released at once into the custody of the bearers in order that he be taken elsewhere for immediate investigation.

Only one more person was needed to drive the car, and as that necessarily had to be somebody thoroughly acquainted with the streets of Paris, neither Dolf nor I could go along on this dangerous trip. Our party left before dawn after the two supposed German officers had rehearsed their parts. They did pretty well shouting their commands in a loud, arrogant way. We prayed that everything would go well.

The time seemed to become eternity as we waited, but it was only thirty minutes later that the men returned with Herman. The act had gone smoothly at the police station, but our rescued friend was still suffering from intestinal distress, for on his way to the prison in the Black Maria the night before, he had eaten several incriminating papers.

≫ 7 ≪

My friends and I had returned to Rotterdam to get the ever-needed Todt papers from our printer. The demand for these papers had become so great that the supply of the stolen ones had run out too quickly. As the Cherbourg location had become too hot for our feet, we had decided to have these documents printed by a trusted friend in Rotterdam. So efficient were these copies that groups of sixty people could travel at the same time and not arouse German suspicion.

The night before we were to leave again for Paris, Dolf and I crossed the Maas river to Katendrecht, the Chinese quarter. The river divides the city into the north, which is the city proper, and the south, which has the huge silos, docks, and factories that give a peculiar atmosphere to every harbor city. It was to the south bank that we went this night for a few hours relaxation.

We were sitting in our favorite restaurant, whose proprietor had been the former cook of the Chinese Ambassador to Great Britain, enjoying the Chinese delicacies and marveling at the abundance of food that was brought to us. Such quantities could have been had for only black-market prices elsewhere. A door near our table opened and Mr. Lao, the proprietor himself, came out and, recognizing us, stopped at our table.

"It is good to see you again. You have been busy?" He bobbed his head and smiled at us.

"There's always work to do," Dolf answered.

"Now don't forget," Mr. Lao leaned over and spoke confidentially to us, "Madame has asked you to come to our house if you ever need a place to hide. Your friends are welcome, too." He turned to go. "The food is all right?"

Dolf and I assured him enthusiastically that the meal was

delicious and thanked him for his generous offer. When we left, Dolf said: "We might be safe from Nazis in his house, but those trap doors into the river are a little dangerous, don't you think?"

"I know they've been dangerous to a lot of German soldiers who have been found floating dead in the river. You can be sure that I would want to be well-acquainted with the layout before I hid in Lao's house," I said.

"It's little wonder that Katendrecht is off-limits now for the German soldiers. They fight a losing battle over here..." Dolf stopped suddenly as he looked off into the room. "Say, Koert, here comes Chris."

I saw him limping toward us. He was a large, strong man, and a man the Nazis would like to have their hands on. He was a valuable worker in the underground and had made a long line of contacts for smuggling our people to England. Chris Lindemans, alias King Kong, was the guide who was to have gone with me on my first train trip to Paris. I had known him for a long time and knew his weakness for women and money as well as his strength and fearlessness of the enemy.

He greeted us warmly as he approached the table. "Well, I see you two are back again!"

He sat down with us while we finished our meal, and then we went to the cafe next door for a few beers and some "American" music. The low-ceilinged nightclub was jammed with young people and clouded with heavy smoke. A Negro band was playing the latest American song-hits imported over the forbidden ether waves to radios hidden in dark and secret places in the homes of the faithful. What a difference between this jazz band and the sentimental, nauseating orchestras of the Nazis.

A tall Negro was just finishing a solo on his trombone when the band abruptly stopped playing. Two German officers had walked in and were pushing their way through the now silent youthful crowd to the bar. The two men stared around as if looking for somebody, then they walked to the door and went out. In spite of their uniforms and their superior *"Gott mit uns"* attitude, I could see that they felt uneasy as no one in the crowd had cast a glance their way, and those lining the path of the Nazis had turned their backs on them. Nothing was so painful to the proud German officer as to be considered as air by the people who, according to their Teutonic minds, should be crawling in the dust at their feet! Chris was mumbling to himself after the officers had left, and he seemed to have become very depressed. Then he spoke to us. "I would like to strangle every Nazi with my bare hands. They have taken my wife; she was in their prison. They would have killed her, but for one thing... our child will be born in prison." Chris put his head down on the table and began to sob. It was pitiful to see this powerful man so overcome.

A short time later I met Chris' wife in Paris after she had escaped her prison. I admired her for her courage after the ordeal she had been through. She told me how her father had given his life to save her and her still unborn child. He had thrown himself against the electric wire surrounding the camp, breaking the circuit and allowing his daughter and two other prisoners who had accompanied them to escape.

Then after the war when I returned from Germany in 1945, I learned of Chris' tragic end — and his even more tragic capitulation to the Nazis. In April 1944, Chris' brother, Henk, who kept the Dutch side of the underground chain going in three countries, had been arrested and after a short trial was sentenced to death. Chris, however, stepped in at the last moment and prevented his brother's death by promising to work for the Gestapo. After that, wild and terrible rumors were spread about this disgraceful traitor. One of the worst things said about him was that he had betrayed the Allied paratroop landing at Arnhem, Holland, but this rumor was false because Chris had been arrested by the Allied troops in Belgium at the time that the northern part of Holland was still occupied by the Nazis. From there he was shipped to England where he was kept in the Tower of London. Later he was brought to the same prison in Scheveningen, Holland, where his brother had been held previously — the notorious "Oranje Hotel." Here Chris was not allowed to see anyone, not even his wife or brother with whom I tried to visit him. My offer to testify in his behalf was refused. Before his trial he became seriously ill, and according to the newspapers he took poison, which a nurse was said to have smuggled in to him.

But now as he sat and drank with us so companionably, he was the trusted Chris with a heart of gold, the Chris who was not afraid of anybody, not even of the Germans who had forbidden him further admission to the whole of the Atlantic Wall zone. He did not pay any attention to their ban; he knew too many compromising facts about most of the German officers who were stationed in Cherbourg and he knew that they feared he would talk to their superiors. Chris would drink them under the table, but not before they had put their signatures to some valuable documents.

The band had started to play "Tiger Rag," so Rotterdam's youth had temporarily forgotten its everyday tribulations, enthralled as it was by the intoxicating rhythm; Chris, Dolf and I ordered another round of beer.

❧ 8 ❧

The next morning we were on the train from Rotterdam to Paris. It was the same trip I had taken so fearfully months ago, but this time I knew the procedure better as I had made several of these runs since then. My friends, Herman and Dolf and I had said a final farewell to our families. We were going to try to cross the Pyrenees mountains before the end of the year.

Our train at this moment stood in the Feigny station awaiting the French customs. Unlike on my first trip, the orders were now that the baggage and papers of even "the faithful laborers of Todt" had to be examined. We had to wait a long time for the customs officials to get to us. As we were talking together in the waiting room, someone from behind me took hold of my arm. I turned to look squarely into the smiling face of a man in the uniform of the Sicherheits Dienst — the S.S. Security Service!

"Follow me!" he ordered.

With one look I said good-bye to my friends. I was alarmed, for I had no hope of getting through the search for which I was undoubtedly headed. The briefcase in my hand held the evidence against me. I picked up the rest of my luggage and followed the officer through the station into a small room. After we were in, the agent locked the door, then turned and asked:

"How much money have you got?"

"Five hundred francs. I just exchanged them at the Dutch border," I replied. There were also two thousand guilders in my briefcase, but it was his job to find them. It was for such an emergency that I had put them in a hollowed-out bar of shaving cream. These S.D. officers were supposed to be experts at their jobs and were noted for their cleverness and thoroughness. Now I could see how much truth there was in these rumors.

"Well, show me the money," he barked.

I took my wallet out of my pocket, but before I could get the money out of it, he snatched it from my fingers. At that I became uneasy, for if he scrutinized the papers in my wallet, he would certainly detect the forgeries. While he was looking through my papers, I tried to control the panic that was rising in me. I kept staring at the gun that protruded from his hip pocket. I could scarcely overcome the urge to grab it and try to escape. I could probably overcome the officer, but I would not be able to get past the men at the gates. Violence would do no good here, so I waited anxiously while the man went through my things. Nothing in them had caused any comment. It was time for a few prayers of hope.

Now he was looking at my Dutch identification card. If only I had disposed of it as I intended! On the card I had been named first as a "student," then as a "doctor" when I thought I had a chance to escape to Sweden on a German boat, and finally as "office clerk" for my escape to France. In addition to these changes I had covered the traces of words left by the ink eradicator with ink spots. It would surely arouse his suspicion. He slowly pulled it out of its case, and, asking my name and address, compared them with the information on the card. Then I prayed again. It helped: just when he had pulled the card so far out of its case that another pull would have brought the ink spots into view, he jammed it back into the case. It had not given me away! Next the agent examined my clothes. I paid particular attention to the places on my body he did not search, for I might need this information later. He completely unpacked my large pieces of baggage, and his hands were quick as he looked at and handled every one of my belongings. He looked at both sides of every blank page in a writing pad, and he even shook vigorously the army tins of food I was to use on the mountain trip.

Then I was allowed to go back to the train. I still had the bottle of gin for a friend in Paris, and more wonderful, I still gripped my briefcase, which had remained unnoticed and unopened! When I returned to the train, my friends stared amazed as I returned to the compartment. I collapsed on the seat. The fear that I had held in during the search now shook me from head to toe. I limply put the briefcase on the floor against the seat. It held the precious travelling papers of Todt, a list of underground workers' names written in my own code, and documents that revealed my anti-Nazi sympathies!

When my friends and I reached Paris, we went immediately to visit Jules Mohr and his wife in their villa outside the city. Before the war Mohr had been director of the K.L.M., the Royal Dutch Airlines in Paris, but since the fall of France, he was a temporary director with the Red Cross. In this strategic position he could cover up his underground activities. He shipped many people to Switzerland and to the Haut-Savoye and the Pyrenees mountains, where they joined the Maquis, the armed resistance troops. It would have been easy for my friends and me to join their forces with Mohr's help, but after long consideration we had decided that we could be more useful in our present resistance work.

Every time we spent a day at the Mohrs, we enjoyed their unlimited hospitality, and in the quiet of their home we were able to forget for awhile the nervous tensions of our daily lives. We relaxed from the constant anxiety that hounded us in our work. Little did we know as we sat around the big fireplace enjoying each other's company that we would, before too long, be together again in the dreadful atmosphere of Buchenwald concentration camp. Jules Mohr died there in 1945 at the time my friends and I were prisoners.

It was at the Mohrs that we met Betty, the wife of the former Dutch consul in Perpignan, a little town at the foot of the Pyrenees mountains. Betty had been a house guest of the Mohrs ever since she had been released from prison at Fresnes in Paris. When I first met her, I could see that she had been suffering and was still laboring under great emotional stress. The Mohrs told me that her husband was now a prisoner at the concentration camp of Compiegne, north of Paris. She had previously been able to visit him during his stay at the Fresnes prison, but since his transfer to

Compiegne he was allowed to see no one. Prisoners in Compiegne were considered dangerous political people and accordingly no longer fit to receive any of the small favors that even convicted murderers and other criminals were granted.

Betty was in despair and felt remorse, as she knew well that she had been the sole cause of her own, as well as her husband's, arrest and misery. Whenever my friends and I were in Paris, we took Betty out to try to cheer her up, and every time she would tell us the story of the arrest and how she was the cause of it. She told it over and over in detail as though it relieved her to live it again. The first time she told us, we were in the Chinese restaurant behind the Care Luxembourg, having dinner with a few Allied flyers.

"You know," she began, "how for many months Paul and I had been able to get people out of France to Spain with forged papers and our trusted guides. Last fall we had to get out of France ourselves, and we planned to use our own route." Betty stopped and seemed to be lost in thought.

My friend and I waited, saying nothing, knowing that she wanted to talk.

"It was such a beautiful autumn morning, and a good day to start our trip," Betty went on. "We were in the small village in the Pyrenees, the same little place where Paul arranged for so many others to meet their guides. It was our turn to escape now, and we were to meet our guide in a few minutes."

Nervously she twitched her lips as if in pain, but then continued her story. "I suggested that we go into the inn and wait. Paul ordered wine for us, and no sooner had we started to drink it when two German mountain police entered the inn. I suddenly became very nervous and couldn't seem to control my fear. But the police were very polite and asked for our identification papers, which Paul gave to one of them.

"The German looked at the papers and, saying everything was in order, turned to go. But the other policeman stopped him and said: 'I think something's wrong here — look at the glass shake in the lady's hand.'"

Betty fingered the fork at her place. "I felt as though I would collapse completely — I don't know what happened to me. The two police and Paul looked at me, and I shook even more. I watched in despair as the Germans started searching Paul, for he had compromising papers strapped to his leg. I knew that we would never make the trip we had sent so many others on.

"As the Nazis took us out the door of the inn, we saw our guide waiting, leaning against a building. He barely glanced at us, then picked up his rucksack and walked away — alone.

"On the way to the police station I could hardly stand the strain of knowing it had been my fault. Hadn't I been in trouble before, that I could not be calm when two officers merely inspected our papers? Why did I have to be afraid just then? Now Paul is in Compiegne, and I'll never see him again and I put him there!" Betty put her face in her hands in desolation. It had been many months since her husband had been arrested, but the pain of knowing she had caused it would never heal.

"He will be out of there, Betty. Everything is being done to get him out," my friend said, trying to make her feel better. But we all knew that if he did get out, it would be a miracle.

Three months later my friends and I were prisoners in the Compiegne camp with Paul, and from there were with him on the transport to "Dora," the underground death commando, where he died six weeks later from the gruelling work on the V-bomb.

❧ 9 ❧

Dolf, Herman and I had been working in the French underground for months. It was now October, 1943, and we knew that we could not get through another winter in France without being detected by the Nazis. We made arrangements to leave on the very next escape transport through the Pyrenees mountains on foot to Spain. The snow that was due would make the already difficult trip more hazardous and perhaps even cut off our flight. So we were anxious to go as soon as possible.

Just before we were to leave, however, several people from Holland arrived in Paris to make this same trip to Spain. It was expedient that some of us give them our place in the transport. We were already well situated in the city and could stay there a few more weeks without too great danger, but the newcomers would have had to acquire food and money and French identification papers if they had not gone on immediately. So it was that the last transport to successfully cross the mountains left without us.

Work was still to be done in Paris. A young Dutchman, having tampered a bit too much with ration cards, came to us for help. After sheltering him a few days at "Madame Rouge's," we were lucky enough to bring off his escape.

A few days before leaving Rotterdam, I met a man in the Hague who was the leader of an organization which smuggled people to England in Dutch fishing boats. As these boats could not return, there had been so few boats left that he was having difficulty getting people to safety. Every day the number of those to be delivered from the Nazis increased. When I offered him the opportunity to get his charges to France by making use of our stolen, reprinted Todt Organization papers, he eagerly accepted. As I did not have the time to bring him in direct contact with our

45

men who would put the refugees on the train in Rotterdam, we arranged a way for him to prove his reliability. We agreed that he would ask the BBC in London to play a certain tune on one of their programs on a certain day and at a certain time. Though I had good reason to be convinced of the man's trustworthiness, I could not expect my friends to believe me implicitly. So I told them what tune would be played, and when they heard it, they would know everything was in order.

Early one chilly morning, two Allied fliers entered our little room in the south of Paris. They had been shot down over Dutch territory after their famous and successful flight over the Moehne dam in the Ruhr area. The moment I saw Sydney Hobday, English navigator, and Frank Sutherland, Canadian rear-gunner, with our Todt papers and heard about their connections with the man from the Hague, I knew our plans had been successful.

To avoid an embarrassing situation at the border, as neither of them spoke or understood French or German, the two fliers had been specified on their papers as deaf and dumb. But once in Paris their tongues were loosened and their ears were opened. Frank was very quiet, though, and he had a peculiar absent-minded stare. Sydney told us that he had suffered a rather severe shock when their plane razed the tops of the trees when they had been forced to an emergency landing in Holland. Frank still saw the trees coming toward him.

Sydney and I had a pleasant stroll that afternoon from the Louvre over the Champs Elysees to the Arc de Triomphe, where we paid a short tribute at the tomb of the Unknown Soldier. There we stood looking at the restless gas flame always burning. An Englishman and a Dutchman brought together for a moment in France by a whim of fate, soon to go our own ways again. Where to? Only God knew.

I wondered what the German soldiers who were standing next to us were thinking. Did they, too, see the accusing finger of the soldier whose remains rested under the marble? Did they, too, hear his voice, as I did, that asked us why we could not live together, as free men, in peace and happiness? His life had been given in vain because it had not taught those who came after him that peace, liberty, and happiness could be found only in God and His commands — love your neighbor as yourself. I sighed and prayed that the unknown soldier of World War II might be a more successful reminder.

At last there were no more obstacles. The necessary connections between Holland and Spain had been readied again and finally we were aboard the train to the south of France the night of October 21st.

Sydney and Frank were safe in the able hands of our friend Thys van Rogge, to whom should go most of the credit of having organized the underground route from Paris to the Spanish border. Thys was one of the many who would never see the end of the war — he was fatally wounded in the Allied bombardment of Buchenwald. Long after the end of the war, we heard that Sydney and Frank had safely escaped to Spain and that many others had used the same route to safety. Only we had failed and had fallen into the hands of our enemies. Our work had been ended too early; our accomplishment was little.

That night there were twelve of us passing the former line of demarcation between unoccupied and occupied France near Dijon. Examination by the Germans was superficial. Our papers said we were going to work for the Germans at Marseille. Early next morning at the station of Avignon we divided into two groups; the one that Herman, Dolf and I were in took the train to Lourdes, where we arrived late that same night.

A password admitted us to the Hotel Caillet. The proprietress and her daughter, both of whom we would learn to be fearless patriots, received us cordially. We sat down at a table with a group of American and English fliers, Polish officers, and French civilians who were having a delicious dinner. We would need the nourishing food for our pilgrimage which was not this time to the grotto of Our Lady on the other side of town, but over the forbidding mountains to Spain. We spent two nights and a day in this hospitable house before we set out on our hard climb.

Sunday morning in the deepest darkness, George, the leader

of this part of the trip, my two friends and I left the house as the
first to go to the place of departure at the foot of the mountains.
The others would follow in small groups during the day. We went
by train to Puzac, a tiny village where an old woman gave us a
hearty meal prepared on an old open fireplace. When we left
there a few hours later, the rain was pouring down. We asked
George if the rain here did not mean snow high up in the
mountains. He thought it was too early in the year for snow. It
would prove to be a fatal miscalculation!

The darkness began to fall over the lonely country road as
we walked along to our rendezvous. Only once did we stop.
George whistled. A man crawled out of the bushes alongside the
road. He did not look very happy and with good reason — he was
drenched to the skin. However, without a word he began to hand
each of us several pieces of baggage that had been hidden in the
bushes. We learned that the rest of our group had passed this
point earlier in the day and had left their belongings. As they had
to pass a little town about one mile further up, they would have
attracted undesirable attention with so much baggage.

George had timed our trip well. It was almost completely
dark when the five of us, heavily loaded, quickly made our way
through the little town.

When we reached the hut where the others were waiting for
us, the night and the curtain of rain made vision impossible. Even
inside the hut, no light was permitted. The last instructions were
given in a whisper, then we were ready to start the trip. Two
French guides led the line of the thirty-four refugees. Our party
was made up of Americans, Englishmen, Frenchmen, Poles,
Dutchmen and Tunisians — one of whom was a woman. Another
French guide walked last in line.

What thoughts crossed my mind as we began this final lap
of our escape! For most of us it meant the beginning of the end of
many years of oppression and a chance at the freedom we had
longed for. Only during the past years, since the curse of Nazism
had come over us, had we realized what a great blessing it was to
be free. Freedom from persecution, freedom from fear, and

freedom of opinion had been words empty of meaning until what they stood for was taken away. But now we had a chance to find our precious freedom, and then to return to fight for the freedom of our families and our countries. That was my goal, and for only a few moments did I ever think of the dangers that were between me and that goal.

The way would be hard with a climb of ten hours the first night, a day of rest, and again a climb of eight hours the last night. Then we would be in Spain where the Gestapo could no longer drag us off to their prisons.

Only the day before, George had shown us the letters of the Dutchmen who had taken our place in the previous transport. They described the inhumanly exhausting expedition over mountains thousands of feet high, the climbing and descending past ravines and crevices and the wading through speeding torrents. But they spoke, too, of their immense gratitude and pride that they had been able to come through alive. How they broke down and cried with relief and happiness when they saw the Spanish village, their symbol of freedom.

If we had known that their expedition was child's play compared to the dangers ahead of us, there is no doubt that we all would have immediately returned to try another way, if only not to be obliged to go through what forever after we would remember as a terrifying nightmare.

I doubt if I, or anyone else on that ill-fated trip, can give an accurate account of the next days and nights in the mountains. Often in the future I was to come face to face with death, but never again would it have such a profound effect on me as in those hours when we were so close to our freedom. The terrific contrast between freedom and death, between everything and nothing, filled the succeeding hours with unbearable suspense. Later, when I was in the hands of the S.S., the idea of death would be too familiar to frighten me anymore. Then I knew that nothing could be expected any longer, and that escape from their powerful grip was almost impossible.

We started full of hope and courage. Our footsteps sounded

dull and hollow as the way led over a paved road. Then our feet sank deep into the thoroughly water-logged grass fields or slipped on gravel-covered paths. Occasionally, we would pass some lone houses, and we would proceed more quietly. But in the starless night, the endlessly falling rain, all noise could not be avoided. It was hardly possible to see the person in front of me, and I was constantly bumping into him. When I managed to get behind someone in a light-colored raincoat, I was able to distinguish faintly a white patch to guide me. It was easier than walking with my arms stretched out in front of me.

Our rest period was five minutes every hour. We were drenched to the skin from the beginning, so sitting or lying on the wet grass did not make us any wetter than we were. After our rest, we started off at a faster speed. The way became more difficult. We were falling into ditches and scrambling over barbed wire fences which tore our clothes. Higher and higher we climbed, wading through mountain streams, falling over huge stones which would begin to roll down the slopes, and clutching at the branches of the bushes which kept swinging in our faces.

Further and further, higher and higher, we climbed. Already I wished desperately for the night to end so I could sleep all day. Suddenly I became aware of the fact that the rain had turned into snow, which clung to our wet clothes. I remembered that George had told us that we would have to climb as high as ten thousand feet!

The first signs of fatigue became visible. We had to wait for stragglers more frequently, the rest periods had to be longer, and some of us abandoned what little baggage we had tried to carry.

The snow became drier higher up. It was a relief to be out of the soaking rain, but it was a relief of the mind, as our clothes were already saturated. Only the guides, who wore large rain capes, had a dry thread on their bodies.

At least we had the comfort of knowing that our route was safe from the Germans. Hundreds of refugees had gone the same way without ever having been detected, because the way was high and difficult where no regular patrols could be made by the

Germans. And especially in weather like this they would not be on the lookout. I tried not to think of the fact that this route never had been used in the wintertime.

We had walked for hours and I had lost all idea of time. It seemed to me that I had been walking so all my life. I was virtually in a trance with only one desire — to reach freedom. The snow made it easier to see our companions, so we were no longer afraid of colliding with each other in the darkness. Gradually the night turned into day, which meant the end of our grueling march. I thought happily of a fire and a bed. But it became lighter even though the sun could not penetrate the lead grey sky. And still we trudged on. I could see no canteen, which was to be our refuge during this day. I became uneasy.

Could the guides have lost their way? Hesitantly that thought arose in me, to be immediately scorned and thrust down. Impossible! That must be impossible! To lose our way in this cold, white, deserted, inhospitable world of towering mountains, deep ravines, unfathomable precipices, without cover against the whipping snow and the icy cold — no, that could not be! But the guides moved uncertainly; with grave eyes they looked at each other and spied searchingly in every direction and at every snow-covered mountain ridge. Then we would start off again in another direction. I looked at my friends. I hoped they had not discovered yet the awful truth, but I could see in their tired eyes that they had.

The snow became even thicker and hid the roughness of our path. At times we climbed like chamois up the steepest mountain slopes to find on the other side far beneath us a wide, ice-covered mountain lake. Then down again we would slide, grasping bushes and stones to break our speed. What a sad group we were! Not one of us was dressed for this cold weather. We could scarcely believe that only a few days ago we had been strolling in Paris under the warm autumn sun.

The woman wore a light summer coat, thin stockings, and low shoes. The three Polish fliers, who had spent four years in German prisoner of war camps before they had escaped in Cologne, had neither coats nor baggage. With their hands in their pockets and their shoulders pulled up high they climbed on without showing a sign of fatigue. They were an inspiration to the rest of us. It was obvious that they were accustomed to these climbs in their Polish mountains as they told us later. We poor Dutchmen, who had hardly ever seen a mountain, exerting all our strength could not help but lag behind.

It seemed impossible that some of us could go on. I felt that I must give up if our goal was not reached soon. This was the time to break into my box of Benzedrine. I had thirty tablets of this strength-restoring drug. If it could help a soldier in combat, it would help a Dutchman get over the mountains! I took three tablets, and distributed the rest to those who seemed to need it most.

After fifteen to twenty minutes I slowly regained my strength and it was miraculous, not to say alarming, to see how powerful I felt. It was as if I had not been on my feet climbing these last twelve hours, but as if I were just beginning the march. No trace of fatigue remained. The mountains had lost their horrors, and the world and the future appeared bright again. Helping and supporting others, carrying some of their belongings, I felt indestructible, a young god. If only now luck would be with us and we could reach the canteen before nightfall, I knew I would be saved for the present. The action of this precious drug could not be expected to last longer than seven to eight hours.

It became afternoon and our march continued on through the ever falling snow. Repeatedly the guides urged us to go faster. The thought of another night in this terrifying wilderness drove us forward. The desire for freedom was no longer our main concern, but instead the need for a bed and some warm food.

Mountain huts would often loom up in the distance, but with bitter disappointment we would discover them to be stacks of moldered wood. These optical illusions certainly did not improve our morale.

A dog barked. Certainly this would mean that men were near to help us. But still we went on. The solitude became unbearable.

Suddenly we did see a hut, a real hut! Scarcely noticing that daylight was fading we hastened to it. The inhabitants refused to help us and would not even give shelter to some who were at the end of their strength. However, the hut had enabled the guides to orientate themselves, and they assured us that the canteen was not far away.

Since the Benzedrine tablets had already lost their effectiveness I decided to take a few more, but then remembered there was not a single one left. Almost despairing, yet determined to reach the canteen, I dragged myself along with my two friends. The guides had already disappeared from sight. They left their footprints in the snow to lead us. The day was waning fast and fear of the darkness doubled our efforts.

All at once I had an extraordinary experience, one that I had read about in studies on parapsychology. It is called by the French "*la vision du de'ja vu,*" literally translated it means "the vision of what one has seen before." It may be described as having a vivid impression that one recognizes certain things or objects which one is absolutely sure never to have seen before, neither in reality, nor in pictures.

We were close to our goal, although this was not yet apparent, when I had an abrupt feeling that the surroundings, hitherto so hostile, were familiar to me.

"Come along!" I called out. "We are right! Follow me!" Herman and Dolf looked at me in astonishment and probably feared that I had lost my mind. After dashing down the steep mountain slope holding on to the branches of the trees, I waded through a wild streaming torrent to see a rather large lake with a dam. On the left side of the lake was our canteen. It was no surprise to me. On the contrary, I knew it was there!

I opened the door and stepped into the wonderful warmth. The interior of the large dining room seemed very familiar. Every room I went into I recognized. Even the proprietor seemed to have a place in my memory. But I was so exhausted at the time that I thought all this quite natural. Later, in the solitude of my prison cell, I tried to find an explanation for the strange occurrence.

I surmised that because of extreme fatigue, the resistance of the synapses along the nerve paths in the brain had diminished so that a kind of short circuit had been caused. Thus, the optical impulse from the lake, the canteen, and the rooms had made a short circuit to the memory center before reaching the optical center. This, then, would explain my experience of recognizing these objects I had never seen before in my life. But at this time the rare phenomenon held little interest for me. I was too worn out to care, and I began at once to dry my clothes and body by the fire. We had been on our feet a long time. Twenty-one hours we had walked, climbed, stumbled, and fallen. We had conquered mountains almost ten thousand feet high in the most miserable weather conditions. It was an almost fantastic and incredible achievement made possible by our determination to reach freedom and our horror of dying a terrible death in the snow.

I had lost my few belongings that afternoon when I had crashed down a steep mountain slope at a furious speed, first on my back, then on my belly. When I came to my senses, I was surprised and thankful that I was not injured. The first part of our march was ended. It was good to be alive. It was good not to know then what more we were to endure on these mountains.

﹥ *IO* ﹤

It was our plan to remain in the canteen throughout the day and to continue on the next night. The thought of the long sleep I was to get already relaxed me. The three Polish officers, the two Americans and the Englishman had dinner with Dolf, Herman and me. It became a very pleasant meal, especially since the Poles and I had done away with two bottles of sherry before dinner, and now several bottles of red wine decorated the table. Everyone told of his experiences in the war. The Poles told of their short but courageous struggle against the ruthless invader and of their trying times in the German prison camps. Our American and English friends told of their flights over Germany and of their bombardment of German factories and cities. We Dutchmen did not say much — we were not yet out of danger, and it would be better for everybody involved if we were known only as harmless students.

We shared our last cigarettes, which we had dried carefully. We drank to our victory with the delicious wine. Though we exchanged names and addresses, I can now remember only the names of the Americans, Hugh Snyders from Pittsburgh and Tom Aufmouth from somewhere in Wisconsin.

Then we called for more wine, but before it was served, a guide came up to the table.

"Come on, we must be out of here in a few minutes," he said.

Stunned, I glared at him as if he were playing a bad joke. "Go on — in this condition?"

"Yes, we must move at once," was the unbelievable reply. "We cannot run the risk of the Germans visiting us here tomorrow by day. And tonight is the only night we can be sure of passing certain guards safely." I translated these disheartening words to the others who did not know French.

"Impossible! It cannot be," Tom groaned. "My legs are like lead."

The guides were getting impatient. No doubt they would leave us here if we did not make a move at once. I could not understand this sudden change of plans. Why hadn't the guides told us when we first arrived that we would not have our rest? We looked at each other across the table. I could see complete fatigue on the face of each one, and I knew how they felt. "What'll we do?" Hugh mumbled.

"What can we do?" I said as I began to get up. But I could not move. My knees, hips, and shoulders were stiff, and I remained helpless in my chair. The others got up slowly and did not notice my predicament. Then two of the Poles saw me try to stand again, and they helped me to my feet. We left the warmth of our refuge, and with the rest of our group lined up in front of the canteen. The cold wind blew through our damp clothing. It was a miserable feeling. Some of us were nauseated, others swayed so violently that they fell over. Slowly we began to move. A push started me going, and as long as we walked steadily the pain in my joints was bearable. I stepped mechanically, but could stop only by stumbling against the man ahead of me.

Suddenly we stopped. After a few minutes the man ahead turned and whispered to me: "The guides have gone ahead to reconnoiter. We must lie on the ground until the signal."

Not able to bend my knees without severe pain, I rigidly fell forward with my face in the snow. Only my outstretched hands broke the fall a little. Stunned by the shock and the burning pain in my whole body, I waited for the signal that it was safe to go on. Dolf helped me to my feet. From then on I do not remember much of that night. The first hours had been the worst, and the pain eased with the continued marching. I walked as if in a dream, stumbling and swaying but somehow going on.

It was only when the day broke that I became interested in the surroundings again. We stood at one side of a ravine in which deep down water splashed in a wild torrent. Across the ravine were a few houses in the rocky vastness of the mountains. If only I could reach one of them to rest my exhausted body for a few hours! But there was no way of crossing the gaping ravine. Then my mind went back to its dreaming.

At noon I saw the first section of our group stop several hundred yards ahead of me. When I reached them and had dropped exhausted to the ground, the others moved on again. The three guides came over to me.

"Give us your ration cards, we're going back," one of them said.

I was both amazed and happy. "We're in Spain, then?" I asked.

"No, but the Spanish village is behind that mountain there. Since the Frenchmen know the way from here, they can lead you. We have to go back. This trip has taken too long already, and if we don't start back now, we may never get back."

George's advice of not letting the guides leave before we saw the Spanish village with our own eyes ran through my mind. But I was much too tired to make any objections. The guides turned their backs on me and quickly left. After I watched them as far as I could see them, I looked ahead of me at the mountains we were to cross. It would not be long now until I could rest. We had gone thirty-nine hours with but two and a half hours' stop at the canteen.

I got up out of the snow and went on again. This time I felt that every step was taking us closer to our destination. I had regained hope and confidence that we would get through. The prospect of a warm bed and a long sleep pushed me on. After seemingly hours of walking I again fell into my trance. I realized that I was in the midst of the group. Everyone had stopped, and the Frenchmen were talking. I could not believe what I was hearing.

"We are lost! We cannot find a pass," the Frenchmen said.

There we stood staring around us, and everywhere was a

snow-covered mountain hemming us in. Behind one was our Spanish paradise!

A searching party was quickly made of the Frenchmen, who had taken the responsibility in place of the guides for our reaching Spain. The three Polish officers began a search in another direction. The last I ever saw of these indestructible Poles was as they ran along a mountain ridge silhouetted against the clouded sky. Their determination to find freedom and never to suffer in a prison camp again must have given them strength above the natural.

The rest of us — Americans, English, Tunisians, and Dutch — went back a short way to a hut we had passed. I wondered that the Americans and the English did not join the search party. One might expect that, being fliers, they would be in extremely good condition from their thorough training. But our rough experience was too much for anybody. I was surprised enough that we Dutchmen, for whom this had been the first test in mountain climbing, had been able to get this far. I would not repeat it for all the money in the world!

We had been in the hut hardly half an hour trying to make a fire, when we heard cries from outside and far away. "We've found the village! Come on, the soup is ready!"

Our deadly fatigue disappeared all at once, and we rushed outside.

High above us against the mountain slope we saw two people waving and making signs that we should follow them. Higher up, a trail in the snow leading to the ridge of the mountain was discernible. What did it matter that the mountain was as high as those we had climbed the night before. The village and freedom were on the other side. Before the darkness would fall, we should be in safety! The very thought gave me wings. I had been the last in line all day, but now I was the first to start the climb, and soon I was far ahead of the others. I felt no tiredness, and as though I was just beginning the climb, I worked my way through the deep snow. It took two hours to reach the top of that mountain. A valley enclosed by several mountains spread itself out deep below me. Eagerly I looked around for the Spanish village, but in the grey mist that slowly rose up out of the valley, I could not discover anything but a part of a trail in the snow made by the others who had called to us. Taking a few deep breaths, I dashed down with all my energy. Sometimes I slipped in the snow. I jumped over and into many mountain streams. After half an hour of this crazy tempo I had arrived down in the valley. I looked around and saw the Frenchmen coming toward me, retracing their steps. When they got nearer they shouted, "We have made a mistake. It was an optical illusion again!"

Thunderstruck, I stopped, stunned, beaten, despairing. I cannot remember what thoughts came over me. Probably I was unconscious for awhile, as when I came to my senses, the Frenchmen were out of sight. My friend Herman, though, was coming closer, while the group of Tunisians was farther behind him up the mountain.

Waiting for Herman to reach me, I fully realized the hopeless position we were in. We had lost our way, and there was no one among us who could find it. It was growing dark. A storm started to blow, and already I felt the first snowflakes against my face. The cold had become intense. It seemed this time too much to bear. I repeated over and over the prayers I had been saying on this terrifying trip.

Everywhere around me I thought I saw houses or huts, but these, too, were the same illusions we had had before. I knew it would be useless to go on into the unknown. The only thing to do was to return the way we had come, and spend the night in the hut on the other side of the mountain. At least there we would have protection against the snow and the cold and the darkness of night that was descending over us. A terrible fear came over me. I could feel the grip of death enclosing me.

My friend came up to me and I called out, "Herman, we are lost again!" His face turned grey for a moment. Then he turned around and cried, "Come on, Koert, quick to the hut — it is our only salvation."

I followed. Just then the rest of our group appeared on the

mountain ridge against the sky. Herman and I tried to make them understand by waving that they should return. They turned around and disappeared again on the other side of the ridge.

Fear of death drove me on. Half way up the mountain Herman and I overtook the Tunisians. One of the men lay motionless in the snow. He was at the end of his strength and had given up. His body could suffer no more. The woman cried piteously:

"Max, get up. You will freeze here."

The man made a last try to raise himself, but fell back with a sigh. His companions tried to help him, but he was too heavy for their weakened bodies. They turned and followed along the trail they had just come. The man on the ground cried a few times, then was quiet. Death by freezing does not seem to be cruel. To stand by helplessly was agonizing.

How I ever reached the mountain ridge I do not know, but somehow I got there. I had lost sight of Herman, who in spite of a partially amputated foot had made the terrific climb quicker than I had. By now it was dark, and a heavy snowstorm roared in all its fierceness. Never before had I felt so miserable and dejected. Lost three times in a wilderness with freedom so near and yet so unattainable and far away!

The hut which could save me this night from the death which Max had just found was indiscernible, and the darkness and the blinding storm made it impossible to see the trail in the snow. It would be pure chance if I were to find the hut. I must go faster and still faster if I were to save myself.

Blinded by the storm I started downhill, when suddenly two figures rose up in front of me. It was the two Americans. One of them had sprained his ankle and could hardly stand on his feet. We took him into our midst and stumbled and fell the long way down.

A sudden cry made us stop abruptly. One American had fallen into a mountain torrent which we had not been able to hear nor see in the roaring storm. It took us several minutes before we succeeded in pulling him out of the stream. At last we reached the hut.

A blue, asphyxiating smoke enveloped the small "cabana," which was filled with huddled figures. There was no chimney, and the door was the only outlet for the smoke. We tumbled over the others, to be as near to the fire as possible. We coughed and gasped for air. At times when the noise of the storm subsided for a moment we could hear the terrifying screams of the woman. We took turns going outside to wave a flaming torch to guide her and her companions to the hut. Finally they arrived. The woman's legs were frozen.

No one slept that night. There was not enough room for everyone to lie down. The moaning of the woman sounded continuously in our ears. The smoke of the fire and dampness of our soaked clothes burned our eyes red. Eagerly we waited for daylight, as we expected the Spaniards to come to our aid. It was possible that some of the search party had found the village.

A few hours after dawn we saw a group of men approaching in the distance. We waved frantically to draw their attention, but though they saw us they did not wave back. We had not expected this from temperamental people like the Spaniards. When they got nearer, we saw that it was the Frenchmen of our own expedition. They had not found the village, but had become lost in the storm. In order not to freeze to death they had walked around in a circle all night long. Thus they had at least stayed alive until morning, but now they were at the end of their strength. It was no wonder; they had been on their feet and on the move for almost fifty-eight hours at a stretch. It was an almost impossible and inhuman achievement!

❧ *11* ❧

Our little "cabana" could not hold us all with the new arrivals. The two Americans, the Englishman, and we five Dutchmen, miserable as we were, went out again into the deep snow to another hut, about two thousand feet down the mountainside. Our way was slow, and even the bitter cold could not hurry our tired bodies.

Finally, having reached our refuge, we made a fire from three wooden beds there which were used in the summer by the shepherds. Breaking up the cots completed our exhaustion, and we collapsed on the bare earth floor to sleep a long deep sleep. The second day we spent huddled together or beating ourselves to keep from freezing. Two slices of bread were the only food that day. The next day we boiled grass, but it was so repulsive that we could not swallow it, hungry as we were. We ate our last bread then. Our last hope of reaching Spain was gone, too, for it would be a miracle in the vastness of the Spanish Pyrenees to find people who would give us food and shelter.

Yet in spite of the danger of losing their way and of having no food or warm clothing, two of the Dutchmen decided to go on to Spain. To us it looked as if they were headed for certain death. We heard with happiness later that they had made it. When they reached Spain, they told the people in the village there about us, but the villagers refused to go to our help and refused to let our friends return to direct us back.

The six of us who did not risk the seemingly more hazardous trip south decided to go back down the mountain we had come up to find the houses we had passed during the second night of our climb. We thought there might be some Frenchmen there to guide us. It was our last chance. The winter was closing in, and each day would be more bitter, and the storms more wild.

It was Friday, October 29th, when we started our descent. We went in single file. As I looked around the great expanse of whiteness, it seemed impossible to find help anywhere, but it also seemed that we would at least not be found and captured by a German patrol. After a few hours of tortuous going, I looked down below us and saw two men dressed in green. I broke our silence to tell the others. We stood still and watched. The men below us stopped, too. We went on again and they also moved, though away from us. They had evidently seen us.

So our deliverance from a death of starvation and exposure was near. The thought was good, but I hated myself for it. These men were Nazis — the very ones we were fleeing! There was no turning back, for back there in the mountains we would find certain physical death. Ahead of us was Nazi imprisonment, the abomination of free men. I thought again of warm food and a warm bed. My body in its needs drained all thoughts of eventuality from me. How we cling to this world!

As I stood there miserably trying to realize what had happened, I suddenly remembered the story a friend had told me in Paris. Alone he had tried this escape to Spain, and after a hard climb he had lost his way, and had wandered aimlessly for days in the snow. A German ski patrol had found him, exhausted and starving, and terrified by the thought of a lonely death. He had been joyful to see the German, this enemy, but also this rescuer. It was hard to understand his feelings when he had told about it. I had said then that to be taken prisoner was worse than death. I had my chance now to stand by my noble words.

As it was evident that we were to be captured, we destroyed our forged identification papers and the documents we were taking to England. We kept our money, as we might have a chance to bribe the two German patrols to help us to Spain. Among the three of us we had fifteen pieces of gold valued at about nine hundred dollars, and four thousand guilders in banknotes.

We prearranged to the smallest detail the story which we

would tell at the inevitable questioning by the Germans. This story had to be such that no suspicions of our real activities would be aroused. We went over it several times and made sure that our descriptions of individuals and places corresponded. All of the time we kept moving to ease the hunger pains in our stomachs, which seemed to ache worse when we knew we would soon have food.

At last we saw the Germans approaching us, only there were not two of them but six or seven. They were armed with machine guns, but most fearful of all, with them was a huge black Doberman Pinscher. One of the Germans shouted to us from a distance:

"Lie flat on the ground and don't move. The dog is quick."

Instantly we were on our stomachs. The remark about the dog had done it, for we were more afraid of his teeth than of machine gun bullets. Our small hope of bribing the two Germans we had seen first was lost now that the whole post had been alarmed. We were frisked for weapons. Then one of them said:

"So you are not terrorists. You are just refugees. Get up and come with us. We would like to know a little bit more about this."

We got to our feet and achingly marched under guard away from our freedom. Our captivity had begun — our flight had ended. How different it was from the way we had planned it! It was no longer necessary for us to remember the code messages to be broadcast over the BBC to tell our families of our arrival in England. In Barcelona waited my Spanish friends of school days in Oxford: I had thought of their hospitable home many times during the long hours of climbing. How eager I had been to make my tentative visit with them!

We did not have to go far before we came to a few houses. As we passed by some bushes where some children were playing, Herman let his gold coins slide from his hands into the snow. Perhaps the children would find them in the spring thaw. My friend would never need them again, but we did not know that then. Four months later he succumbed to the S.S. executioners. He was the third death in one family. In October, 1941, his mother and brother had been killed during a night bombardment by the R.A.F. on Rotterdam. At that time one of his feet had been partly shattered by shrapnel, but in spite of this handicap, and under great pain, he had taken the terrible foot march over the mountains and had kept up with the rest of us. He had been able to endure these hardships, but he could not stand the cruel labor on the German secret weapon, the V-bomb, deep under the earth. Exhaustion, starvation, and illness had brought the end of his young promising life. But I wondered if there was not more to it than this, for shortly after our liberation I examined the records of the deceased which had been so carefully made by the Germans. His record said, "Deceased on the twenty-seventh of February, 1944, at four o'clock in the morning, of pneumonia." On the following page I saw the name of another Dutchman. His record said, "Deceased on the twenty-seventh of February, 1944, at half past four in the morning, of pneumonia." I had known him, too; he was a sailor and strong as no other. These suspicious records gave me much to think about...

As we reached the doorway of the police building, I almost felt compelled to turn and run, but I knew there was not a chance of getting away. If there ever was a time of asking God to help me say, "Thy will be done," this was it. I had tried with all my being to escape to freedom and I had failed. I was a prisoner. This was the way it was to be.

The German mountain police were decent enough to give us a simple but copious and warm meal as soon as we reached their headquarters. We ate at a bare wooden table underneath a life-sized picture of the "Fuehrer." It did not take us long to finish, and then for a small dessert we shared a can of condensed milk in brotherly fashion. Hugh Snyders entertained us and helped our spirits and digestion by his optimism and his humorous stories. It seemed impossible that we could laugh, but we did.

Hugh was the first to be taken upstairs for questioning. He was gone only a short time, and when he returned, his clothes were in disorder, and he looked as though he had been searched. Immediately Dolf asked to be allowed to go to the men's room. I followed suit. In spite of the armed guard in front of the open door, we disposed of our roll of Dutch money. It was the most expensive visit I ever paid to a men's room!

Just before dusk, as we sat waiting for the last one of us to be questioned, the French and the Tunisians, who had remained in the hut higher up the mountain, were brought in by the police. They looked completely miserable as they stumbled into the room. We must have looked the same way when we had come in some hours earlier. The pitiful spectacle they presented made me understand again the feeling I had had earlier in the day and which, now that my physical needs had been satisfied, I had already come to regard as unbelievable. This was the feeling that it did not matter to be captured as long as I could have some food.

Our original group was complete now except for the Poles and the two Dutchmen. After the new arrivals were given some food and put through a short questioning, we all were ordered into an open truck. We were guarded by several heavily armed policemen from Arreau, which was our destination.

Here, in a large room of a hotel that was being used as headquarters for the German Police, we waited for the Police Commander. When he arrived, he was obviously displeased at having been called away from a pleasant engagement. He looked at us in disgust and began the ordeal of questioning by ordering the Americans to stand before him.

I listened carefully to the questions and the answers of the others, so that I could prepare my own replies. Finally I stood before the brutish Commander. He glared at me and asked: "Were you going to England to join the army?"

"No, no — absolutely not!" I vehemently replied, as had all my companions.

"I do not believe you!" he bellowed.

"Why not?" I replied. "I have always read in the German papers that Rotterdam, my home town, was bombarded by the English, so how could you expect me to be friendly to those murderers and to want to join them?" The ambiguity of this remark fortunately escaped him, though it was clear that I had not convinced him yet. I went on to tell him that my medical studies had been interrupted, as he well knew, by the sudden closing of all Dutch universities. My only intention, I said, was to go to Spain to finish my studies there.

The Commander laughed. "I don't believe a word of your story. What good would it be to go to a country whose language you can't speak?" I tried to sound indignant as I answered, "But I speak Spanish fluently!"

This was a tall statement, for I had studied Spanish only superficially, although with my knowledge of French and Latin I was able to read it. I was amazed at my own remark though, and tried not to appear nervous. I thought the man too stupid to disprove my boast, but to my dismay I heard him call for a Spanish interpreter.

Within a few seconds a civilian entered the room. He was to find out if I knew Spanish. With a French accent he asked me several questions in Spanish. Fortunately I was able to get their meaning and answered him at the appropriate times with "Si, señor," or "No, señor," and put in a few other simple words I knew. Finally the interpreter turned to the Commander and said, "This man has a fluent command of the Spanish language."

That fortunately convinced the Commander of the truth of my story, and it almost convinced me, too!

Then the Tunisians were ordered to stand to be questioned. The woman was allowed to sit because of her poor physical condition. As the Tunisians could not speak German, in which the trial was held, an interpreter was used for them. The woman was first to be questioned, and she was asked with whose help she had planned her escape.

"Max," she replied, "one of my countrymen."

The same question was asked of the second Tunisian, and he gave the same answer. The Commander gave an order for Max to be brought before him. No one stirred.

"Where is this Max?" he shouted.

"Max is dead," replied the second Tunisian. "He froze to death in the mountains."

The Commander got red in the face and asked the third Tunisian, "Who was the leader of your group?"

"Max," was the answer.

The Commander's eyes started to protrude, and he roared, "Naturally, also Max. He is dead, and nothing can happen to him anymore. If the next one dares to mention this Max again, I shall beat him to death!"

The last of the Tunisians took his stand, and again the interpreter asked, "Who has helped you plan your escape?"

"Max," he replied unsuspectingly, as the Commander's warning had not been translated.

The Commander almost burst with fury, while we had difficulty keeping our faces straight. Fortunately, however, he did not carry out his threat, but ordered his men to take us away at once.

We were taken to the town of Tarbes in two trucks. At three o'clock in the morning we arrived at the prison, which had fifteen to twenty cells encircling a small inner court. The roof of the court was a brilliant, starlit sky. Two searchlights coldly illuminated the stage of our misfortune. The door of the first cell was thrown open, and before I knew what was happening, I was thrown into the dark interior. The door was closed, the key was turned, and the bolts were shoved into place. Exhausted and prostrate with grief, I fell on the straw mattress in the corner of the cell. I listened to the gloomy noises of clinking keys, creaking bolts and shuffling feet. Then it became silent, distressingly silent. I tried to sleep, but sleep would not come.

One by one the events of this fateful day passed before my burning eyes. This day had brought the turning point from freedom to captivity. I thought of my family, who soon would receive my letter that I had safely arrived in Spain — the letter the guides would have mailed upon reaching Lourdes. I realized that the awful truth could not be kept secret from them for very long. I was glad that for a short period at least they would live in the happy fantasy that I was safe. I tried not to think of the pain they would have when they learned the truth.

I lay there telling myself that there was still hope. I was at least among the living — for that I should be thankful. I did not regret the things I had done. I had known well the serious risks I would run. I had gambled between freedom and imprisonment, if not worse. That I had lost was only incidental. My conscience was clear. I had done my duty to my country and to the freedom-loving peoples of the world.

❧ *12* ❧

Two days I had spent in the prison at Tarbes. I had been able to see my friends and talk with them when we were allowed out in the court to get our food and to wash our faces and hands under the tap. Back in our cells we communicated with each other by shouting. But at the end of the second day no one answered my persistent calls. Then I knew my friends had been taken away. I began to imagine what had happened to them. Had they been questioned by the Gestapo? And if so, were the Gestapo suspicious of our underground activities in Holland and in France? But why had my friends not been put back in their cells?

I thought of all the gruesome stories I had heard about these Gestapo trials, and I could not help shuddering from fear that their beastly methods would be tried out on us. The realization that helping the Allies was punishable only by death did not make me feel any better. The smallest suspicion by the Gestapo of the work we had done would make them try anything to force the truth out of us. I wondered if I could be strong enough to hold out under torture to keep what I knew untold. If I talked, many lives would be endangered. I did not feel capable of the courage I would need.

Most of that night I spent walking restlessly around my tiny cell, at times despairing about the precarious situation I was in, then again praying feverishly for help from God and resigning myself to His will. It was there in the solitude of my prison cell that I first understood fully the wisdom of the first two lines of that simple verse:

> "God and the doctor we alike adore
> When on the brink of danger, not before."

Only much later when I had regained freedom, the signifi-
cance of the last two lines would impress me:

"The danger past, both are alike requited.
God is forgotten and the doctor slighted."

It would all be a lesson never to forget again.

My thoughts in the silence of the night were suddenly
interrupted by the sound of footsteps outside in the courtyard. I
seemed to know they were coming for me. When the key was
turned in the lock of my door, my nerves became tense with
expectation. A flashlight shone in my eyes.

"Get your things and come out," a man ordered.

When the light played around the bare walls of my cell, I
saw that the man was in plain clothes. That meant he was one of
the Gestapo. Would this mean that I was to be tried? In spite of an
intense fear that suddenly came over me, I was glad that something would happen, because now I should soon know what my
fate would be. The uncertainty had become too much to bear. A
gun was pushed into my back, and I was forced into a private car
that waited outside the prison. It was a German-made car, a
D.K.W., which letters we used to stand for "Das Krankenhaus
Wartet" (the hospital is waiting). Even in my anxiety the thought
struck me as quite funny and rather appropriate.

Driving through the dark streets of Tarbes I tried to orient
myself. I had studied carefully an excellent sketch of the town and
its surroundings which a previous prisoner had made on the
walls of my cell. This sketch had reminded me that near Tarbes
was a castle whose occupants had been very helpful to some
friends of mine, and they might help me if I could get away. But
right now it was impossible to move as the man behind the
steering wheel was constantly jabbing his gun into my ribs, and
I could tell that this was not the first time that he had ever handled
this object.

On the top floor of a hotel that served the Gestapo as
headquarters, a few men in civilian clothes were waiting for me.

My first impression of them was that they seemed to be rather decent, but when I had an opportunity to get a better look at their eyes, I felt that I could not expect much good from them. I was shoved down on a small bench while an intensely bright light shining in my eyes prevented me from seeing my examiners. I felt amazingly calm for the time being, and I was able to push away all the terrifying memories of torture that I had heard about.

After the usual introductory questions about my name, address and occupation, I was asked to give an account of my activities which led to my arrest. I started the story my two friends and I had so carefully fabricated. Everything would depend on it, and since my friends had told their stories before me, a slip on my part could be disastrous. So I began slowly.

"We travelled directly from Holland to Paris, where we had spent one night in a small hotel. We never learned the name as we arrived and left there in darkness. From Paris a man named Pierre took us to Lourdes."

I described Pierre accurately according to our previous agreement. This description of course was entirely imaginary as was also the description of Charles, who had helped us from Lourdes. The name of the hotel in Lourdes had been kept scrupulously secret from us, so I was unable to tell it. This was the extent of my story, which was being typed as I spoke. Then the rattling of the typewriter stopped and an impatient voice said:

"Yes, we know all that from the other Dutchmen. I shall write in your protocol to refer to their statements."

My heart jumped with relief. The Gestapo had believed the whole story! The greatest danger had been averted as the death penalty did not apply to attempts to escape to Spain. The story had been beautifully composed. It was full of apparently valuable details that the Gestapo thought might help them in their search for other fugitives. It had been told in a way that made us seem eager to help them in arresting those persons who had taken our money and then had left us in the lurch in the mountains. So convincingly had I told our story that I felt pity for myself, a harmless student who had been betrayed!

Before I was allowed to sign my confession, they first wanted to know exactly where I had been in the mountains and who the guides were who had been with us. Though I was not particularly eager to protect the guides whose fault it had been that we had been taken prisoner, I could not reveal this information, as their arrest might eventually lead to that of many of our friends in Paris and elsewhere. But from the Germans' questions I soon found out to my horror and amazement that they already were too well acquainted with the happenings in the so-called canteen in the mountains. After my questioning by the Gestapo, a German soldier took me to the station in Tarbes to get the train to Toulouse. As we stood waiting on the platform I saw to my distress, the proprietress of the hotel in Lourdes and her daughter, both under German guard. It was a great shock to see them there. Such deep pity toward these two courageous women and patriots filled my heart that I could hardly keep from telling them how sorry I was at their arrest. But feeling had no place here and now. It had occurred to me that this meeting might have been staged on purpose to expose the women. When my guard gave me over to the soldier who was guarding the mother and daughter, I still made no sign of recognition of them. It was possible that they had been arrested only on suspicion and not on certain evidence. But once in the train and on our way to Toulouse, I started an apparently casual conversation with them. I asked them about their arrest and if they had been questioned. They felt free to talk as they told me that the German guard did not understand French. The mother told me that they did not know why they had been taken prisoner. She feared the worst, although they had not been questioned at all.

We tried to encourage each other and to keep from despairing thoughts. I promised never to expose them even under duress as the ones who had harbored us in our flight. Since that day I have not seen nor heard of them again. At the door of the Saint Michel prison at Toulouse we said good-bye. "Que Dieu vous garde," had been their last words to me. May God keep them, too!

Inside Saint Michel prison I was registered and, seeing the

names of Herman and Dolf in the book, I was happy at knowing
we would be together again. But when I asked the German at the
desk to put me in the same cell with my friends, he scornfully
refused. I should have known better than to ask for a favor! I spent
a few hours in an admittance cell and then was taken to the third
floor of one of the large wings of the prison and put in a cell which
was occupied by ten young Frenchmen.

I was glad to have company, and even more so when the
Frenchmen treated me cordially and even shared some of their
precious food with me. I did, however, resent their continuous
talking about food, and I could not understand why they had to
describe from morning until night the details of a certain meal, at
what occasion, at what place, and how it had been prepared or
should have been. Though I had always been able to eat the finest
foods, it never interested me particularly what I ate as long as it
was tasteful and wholesome and contained the necessary calo-
ries. And here where there were so many more important things
to talk about than the steaks, lobsters and oysters of bygone days,
the thought of which only produced an absolutely unnecessary
reflex of secretion by the stomach glands, I sometimes wished for
my solitary cell in Tarbes.

We were allowed to spend fifteen minutes each day outside
in the courtyard, which was surrounded by high stone walls. One
of these times on my way back from the courtyard, I met the two
Americans and the Englishman inside the building. I was so glad
to see them again that I forgot that talking was allowed only in the
cells and in the yard, and I shouted, "Hello, how are you doing?"

Before they could open their mouths, a guard rushed up to
me and gave me a severe beating. When I returned to the cell, my
companions reprimanded me for having brought their cell into
discredit. I still had many things to learn before I would be a good
prisoner! A week after my arrival I was transferred to another cell
in another wing of the prison. It seemed like a promotion because
ten of the eleven occupants there, all elderly Frenchmen, were old
customers who were allowed to receive laundry and food from
the outside. They had plenty to supplement the meager prison

ration of a lump of bread in the morning and some warm water with a few cabbage leaves in the afternoon, but they never offered me anything from their abundant supply.

One day when I returned from the daily airing, I found that more than half of my tiny lump of bread had been stolen. I used to save most of the bread until the evening to be less hungry at night and to be able to sleep better. I could hardly blame the poor fellow who had taken the bread in my absence to ease his hunger. My companions in the cell expressed great pity at my loss as they ate at leisure the delicacies they had received from outside. The only one who offered me his bread was a former valet of a French Baron. As he was the only one who did not receive any extra food, I naturally refused his generous offer. I shall never forget him for it. The others had forgotten what it meant to be hungry. This was my first encounter with men who in their struggle for survival had become completely selfish. I resolved then and there to give from my share whenever I could. I still was not certain that the questioning by the Gestapo in Tarbes had been the final one, and I lived in constant fear of another trial. I had heard that the trials that were held here at St. Michel prison by three expert torturers were inhuman and brutal. I was given evidence of this when one evening the door of our cell was opened, and one of the Frenchmen was summoned to step out. A few hours later that sturdy fellow who had left was returned to the cell a mere wreck, groaning and crying with pain. His arms had been wrung out of the shoulder joints and were tremendously swollen and covered with sweat and blood. Across his back were red welts. The torturers had hung him by the wrists, which had been tied together behind his back. After fifteen minutes he had fainted, but he had been revived with a bucketful of cold water. Then he was hung up again and lashed across the back. But he had not spoken … not yet. Half an hour later he was taken away again, and he never came back.

We kept our morale by telling and believing any optimistic and fantastic rumor that we heard. Everyone refused to regard them as rumors but clung desperately to the pleasant prospects they offered. One of the most popular rumors was that the young people would be forced to join the Todt Organization to work on the fortifications on the West Wall. That certainly was a bright thought, as that would give us a good chance to escape. But unfortunately it was a rumor — nothing more.

After I had been at St. Michel for two weeks, I was again transferred to another cell. I was greatly encouraged to see Herman and Dolf among the numerous occupants. That night we had more food than usual, and it was impossible to eat all of it after the consistently meager portions of the past days. The next morning we were all taken outside, handcuffed two by two, and transported to the station. It was good to be out in the fresh air again, even though we were handcuffed like criminals.

An entire third-class car had been reserved for us in the train to Paris. We certainly appreciated this courteous gesture on the part of the Germans, as all trains were overcrowded during the war. And here we were prisoners enjoying the luxury of a special place to sit on a train! We almost forgot our chains as we sat there looking out of the window at the countryside. Herman was ordered by our guards to tell those prisoners who did not understand German that at certain stations the Red Cross would provide us with food.

We had many stories to tell each other. I was handcuffed to a seventeen-year-old Frenchman, who told us all about his brutal tortures during his trials and showed us the scars that covered his body.

"But how were you able to keep silent?" I asked him.

With deadly contempt in his voice he replied simply, "I hate them, les boches; they have killed my father."

We ate our prison bread in the morning expecting the food from the Red Cross. But nothing came for us, and the rest of that day and evening we had neither bread nor water. Shortly before eleven that night as we neared Paris, one of the German guards undid my part of the handcuff and took the young Frenchman out of the car. He was to be transferred with the two Americans and the Englishman to the prison of Fresnes in Paris. The rest of us were to go on to the concentration camp of Compiegne, north of Paris. The guard forgot to handcuff me to somebody else, so I shoved close to my neighbor and hid my free arm. Here was a chance to get away. I tried to think quickly. I looked around to judge the distance to the door, but as I planned my jump, I knew the train was going too fast. I decided to wait for a better opportunity.

But my chance was gone — another guard assembled us in the corridor in a line and put a long iron over and under each of the handcuffs. I was the last one in the line, and when he saw me by myself, he demanded,

"Why aren't you handcuffed?"

I looked surprised first at my wrists and then at the floor and, shrugging my shoulders, I answered, "Oh, what do you know, I must have lost them."

He snarled and grabbed one of my wrists and put the end of the chain around it, securing it with a big padlock.

By bus we went to the Gare du Nord, so well known to us from our previous visits. I thought again of escape — always looking to be free. Not far from the station I had good friends who would welcome me. Then again to Spain or England! At least my thoughts were free.

On the Paris-Rotterdam train I had another chance to think of getting away. The chain had to be removed from my wrist in order to let the others who remained handcuffed sit down on the benches. However, given this opportunity I could not decide what to do.

There was a possibility that a former German business friend of my father's could help me and my friends. This man held the position of judge in the German Court of Justice at Compiegne. Twice during the war he had made an attempt to visit my father, who on both occasions had refused to receive him. In spite of this, my father had thought it not impossible that this man would be willing to help us if ever we would be in serious danger. Knowing the German mentality and the fact that my father was a prominent lawyer with an international reputation, one could understand that this possibility was psychologically sound. It would be bitter to ask the help of any German, but the concentration camp at Compiegne was the last stop before we would go to Germany where there would not be the slightest chance of escape. So whatever way we could regain freedom now was worth the humiliation, for here in France there was a possibility that we could get away.

I sat there trying desperately to make a choice. I could jump out of the window as soon as the train started up, or I could go on with my friends and help them to escape through the German judge. The first plan was very, very alluring and not at all difficult. I was well acquainted with the huge station and how to avoid its dangerous and guarded places. Not long ago, without making use of my German permits, I had entered and left this station several times one evening without having been discovered.

The second plan was uncertain, but I might be able to get my friends freed with me. So we still sat in the station and I could not make up my mind. It was almost midnight when the train began to move. Then I knew I must get out now or never. I was about to jump from my seat and climb through the window, which I had already lowered, when I looked at my friends and sank back onto the bench. I could not do it. These friends had helped me so often when I needed them, that I could not leave them now that we were in such danger. I rested against the back of my seat and began to eat some food which the kind ladies of the French Red Cross had brought us.

Later I found out that the judge, my last hope of freedom, was no longer in Compiegne, but had been transferred to Rumania. How different perhaps my life might have been if I had known. But thinking back I still am not sure it would have been right to abandon my friends. Though I had been able to be of some little help to my friends as they were to me in moments of material and spiritual need, was I not morally obliged to my family to try in the first place to save my own life, then when possible the lives of my friends?

⇒ *13* ⇐

We were disgusted when we first saw fat "Stalino" sitting on top of his upper bunk in the dark, long, dirty barrack. The huge Italian, who resembled the Russian leader, was frantically searching his body for lice. With steady precision and accuracy his agile fingers, wetted on his lips, were experienced in catching the little insects, which suffered a quick death between the clicking nails of thumb and forefinger. We were disgusted with him at first, thinking that he must be filthy to have lice. But when we, too, started to scratch, we realized that "Stalino" was after all one of the best examples of applied hygiene. Before the lights went out at ten o'clock the first evening of our arrival, I had been able, after careful study of "Stalino's" methods, to catch thirty-seven crawling objects in my shirt! Herman caught thirty-three and Dolf twenty-nine, so we decided that the lice must prefer me to them — a preference I could not appreciate!

We were never entirely free of these pests even after systematic searches of our bodies and clothes and bedding. Until the present day I still think it a wonder that not a single case of typhus had occurred in this camp. If but one prisoner with this disease or one louse infected with the Rickettsia virus had been in the camp, there would have been a terrific epidemic among the thousands and thousands of prisoners.

And so now we were in Compiegne concentration camp. The month we spent there was not too harsh, and it helped to have Herman and Dolf with me, instead of being separated from them as in Toulouse. We suffered mostly from anxiety, waiting for our next move.

In the camp, the French priest-prisoners were allowed to use a small wooden barrack as a chapel. At Mass time the prisoners

79

filled the crude building eager to beg for our Lord's help. Never were such fervent and beseeching prayers said as in that Compiegne chapel, for the dread of being shipped to Germany was always with us. It was a great consolation to me to be able to offer up the sacrifice of the Mass every day and to renew my faith and trust in God. Once in Nazi Germany we would be deprived of all our religious practices.

There was little work to do, and no one was forced to work at this camp. Most of us did cut wood outside the enclosure proper. Some prisoners used the wood to make fires on which to cook the food they received from home. The rest of us sold the wood for a few francs and then bought some precious cigarettes. The cigarette was the symbol of good fellowship, as it was always smoked by a few friends together, each taking a puff at a time, a rather unhygienic procedure but nevertheless very enjoyable. To be offered a puff of an acquaintance's cigarette was a certain proof of his friendship.

We even had a library — and time to read. We were allowed to walk around the spacious grounds, but I remember how foggy and cold was that November weather. The days at Compiegne would not have been too unpleasant if it had not been for the agonizing roll-calls every morning and night. All of the inmates were required to stand while each of the barrack chiefs counted his men. Some days we would stand for hours in the cold wind while the guards searched the camp for a missing prisoner. One day some prisoners had raided the canteen, and one of the Germans went around with a divining rod on his finger searching for the culprits. It was very entertaining to watch him, especially as he had no success. But it was less amusing to find when the roll-call was over, that all the mattresses had been ransacked, and the barracks looked as though a tornado had passed through them.

The food was not sufficient, but it was much better than the food we had eaten in the prison of Toulouse. We had the French Red Cross to thank for that. They supplemented with thousands of kilograms of potatoes and beans the meager rations we were allotted by the Germans. We even received a parcel of food from friends in Paris we had been able to notify of our mishap, but our stomachs had "shrunk" so much in the past weeks that we could hardly eat any of the butter and fat without developing abdominal cramps.

Every night we thanked God that we were still at Compiegne, as we all knew too well that the road out of the camp would lead straight to Germany, the place we never wanted to see as prisoners. Even yet I had some hope to escape as I had been able to convince one of the guards of my honest intentions of wanting to continue my studies in Spain and not of going to England, the worst crime a German could imagine. Slowly I was working on his sympathies and getting his confidence. It seemed that he might be inclined to assist me. But on the twelfth day of December, a Sunday, all prisoners were ordered to gather outside the barracks at noon. We felt uneasy at this sudden order, but we did not expect that the time had come for us to leave. For many weeks there had not been a transport to Germany, and now so shortly before Christmas we thought that there would not be one until after the holidays.

We had been indulging in wishful thinking, for at the first words of the Commander we knew some of us were to be deported. There was still a small chance for us to stay here as only one thousand prisoners were to be shipped. With pounding hearts we listened to the names that one by one were called out in alphabetical order. I did not need to wait long and never was the sound of my name and prison number so hateful to myself. Dolf and Herman shared the same misfortune, and even those prisoners who had been in this camp for many months and who had acquired a certain sense of safety by surviving numerous previous transports were now to go. We had no pity for two young Frenchmen whose names were on the fatal list. They were brothers and had been in the camp a long time. They had a monopoly on the small duties in the camp which entitled them to larger food rations. They were hated by all their fellow prisoners because they never shared a crumb from the packages of food they received almost daily from the outside. They did not even hesitate to grease their leather shoes with butter under the hungry eyes of the other prisoners. These brothers hated us Dutchmen because we had told them many a time that we thought they were shameless, not because of ourselves, as we were not too badly off, but because of their own countrymen, especially the older ones who were in dire need of substantial food.

Even the invalids, including a totally blind Frenchman, were among the thousand whose fate it was to go to Germany. Also to go were the Spanish Communists who had been interned in France since the end of the Spanish Civil War. It appeared to be the beginning of a wholesale transport of all Nazi-hostile prisoners. First Compiegne, the final assembling place in France, had to be emptied to be filled up subsequently with the prisoners from the numerous French prisons. These in turn would be ready to receive the continuous stream of new victims of the Gestapo. It was evident that the Germans suspected the possibility of an Allied invasion on the west coast, and they wanted to reduce to a minimum the number of men able to bear arms for the Allies. I had been thinking sadly of not being home for Christmas, but now I would not even be in Compiegne where there was at least a chapel where I could find some solace at the Mass during this greatest of all feasts. What a terrible fear would fill the hearts of our dear ones at home when they would hear that we would have ended our flight to safety in Germany.

Monday afternoon, in preparation for the transport, the German guards searched the thousand victims for forbidden articles, especially knives and anything that could be used as weapons or tools with which to break out of the train. Taught by experience of previous searches, I was able to smuggle a knife and scissors through this examination. The guard found only my French prayer book, and he was so angry that he hit me on the head with it several times, then tore it to pieces. Perhaps he felt that he was destroying my faith with it, but it had the opposite effect. Every day in the future I was to find out that being thwarted in my religious feelings and convictions was a stimulation to persevere in my belief. If this was not caused by my characteristic Dutch stubbornness, then I can understand a little bit how the holy martyrs in the past had been able to suffer so courageously and without faltering the terrible torture inflicted upon them by their persecutors.

After all of us had been searched, we were put in special isolated barracks for the night. The next morning we marched with about three hundred heavily armed guards through the town of Compiegne, whose inhabitants looked with pity on our dejected group. In a short speech the Commander of Compiegne had promised us a rosy future in his "Fatherland" which — and these were his words — "is so eagerly waiting your help in our glorious fight against the plutocratic-capitalistic-communistic enemy who has so cowardly left your countries in the lurch when Germany had come to protect you." After his fatherly words, we said good-bye with tears in our eyes and promised to behave well on the trip to his beloved country!

At the station a long line of boxcars stopped, waiting for their load. They were to take us to Germany, but before we could get on, we had to be searched again. This time overgrown French S.S. boys did the job. To them the sight of a hair comb was reason enough to give a punishing blow on the head of a helpless prisoner. After this second frisking we were pushed inside the boxcars, and the heavy wooden doors were slid shut. Then we realized what an extremely disagreeable situation we were in. Even the well-known sardines were to be envied in comparison with us, as they could take their crowded position lying down. We had to suffer standing up.

The atmosphere in the car became unbearable a few minutes after the door had been closed. It was difficult to estimate how many of us were in the cattle car, but it was impossible to sit in ordinary rows, for we had figured out by the distance between the iron partitions on the roof of the car, that this could be done by approximately eighty persons. There must have been at least a hundred in there. As soon as the train left the station, we removed the two small glass windows on the sides of the car. It was a welcome if slight relief from the tainted air.

Several prisoners started to investigate the heavy sliding door which had been bolted with iron bolts from the outside. Some of these men had made this journey several times before, and they had always been able to break out of the cars by ingenious methods. Usually they sawed large square holes in the side walls or floor. Dropping through the hole in the floor one had to lie flat on the ground between the wheels of the train as it sped on. That at times somebody was pulverized under those wheels was an unlucky break. There was a sporting chance in this way of escape, and it was one fully worth being taken.

This trip, the men went at the door with knives, chisels, screwdrivers, and drills which they had hidden miraculously in spite of the double search. They worked hard at the door for several hours, until finally they were able to slide it open without difficulty. Another chance to escape was waiting. During the month in Compiegne we had widely discussed the possibilities of an escape during the inevitable train transport to Germany, and we had decided to take any opportunity to make a break. But now that the moment had come, my friends suddenly refused to take this opportunity — which was understandable inasmuch as the landscape that was fleeing by was not inviting to a jump. But my decision was the same as before. Now was our last chance to get away, as tomorrow morning or even that very night the French-German border would be passed. Certainly the Nazis would not help a Dutch prisoner to safety, whereas in France there was a sympathetic population. I agreed with my friends that a jump from the fast-moving train into the darkness was not pleasant, but a German concentration camp was still less so. I counted on my experience in the art of falling which I had acquired during my judo training, but still more on good luck and the help of my guardian angel that I would not be seriously or fatally injured when I landed. I got help from Bernard Norman, the son of a French general who at that time was fighting in North Africa on the side of the English and Americans. He had been my excellent and trustworthy friend since our meeting during the last night of our stay in the prison at Toulouse. With his help I succeeded in persuading my other friends to join us in this last chance of escape. It was dusk by now, and we would have to wait until darkness before we could make our jump. Just as those near the door were to open it, the sound of shooting suddenly rang out. The train slowed down, and the shouting of the German guards and the barking of the dogs was loud in the night. The train stopped. It was not difficult to guess what had happened. The prisoners in one of the other boxcars had been ahead of us. In nervous tension we listened to the turmoil outside. Our hearts were with our fellow prisoners who were now fighting for their lives. Would they be able to get away or would they be hunted down by the dogs? Gradually the commotion died down. Then a few more shots made our eardrums vibrate. We heard a few curses and cries, and then the train started to move again. Every one of my nerves was under a terrific strain. I thought of myself being shot at and hunted and the thought itself was frightening.

We had not considered one thing, one factor that was outside our power and that would destroy all of our plans — the moon. Suddenly the clear, white disk appeared from behind a cloud and threw its white light over the fast-passing landscape. Nature was not in our favor. It had been the snow in the mountains that had covered our road to freedom, now it was the moon that so brilliantly lighted it. Yet a few of the prisoners wanted to make a try to get out. Slowly the door was opened and three men jumped out of the car. But before the last of them could have reached the ground, a salvo of fire from a machine gun rapped out. Again the train slowed down. Undoubtedly the German guards had been posted between and on top of the cars, otherwise such a prompt reaction could not have been possible.

The train stopped, and the guards stood in front of our car before we even had time to close the door. A sadistic laugh rang out, and a drunken voice cried, "Here are the swines that wanted to get away. I'll shoot into the herd." He emptied his gun into our car, and six bullets whistled over our heads as we fell over each other onto the floor.

The Hun jumped into the car, and growling the vilest curses

he started to beat madly the defenseless heap of prisoners with the butt of his rifle. The crying and yelling of the victims mixed with the hollow sound of the strokes on their backs and skulls and with the cracking sound of lashes on bare skin. When the raging guard was exhausted and his companion who had joined him had tired of this brutality, they ordered us to stand up.

"Who forced the door?" one of them demanded in a hoarse voice. Nobody answered.

"How many have jumped out?"

Again nobody answered.

In turn we had to count ourselves, and we got to ninety-seven. They were satisfied; in all probability, all three of the would-be escapees had been killed.

The two guards remained in our car when the train continued on its way. Several men were moaning with pain, and the guards called for a doctor. I waited a moment to see if the French doctor, whom I knew to be in this transport, was in our car, but when no one stirred or replied I climbed over the mass of human beings to the guards. I was ordered to look at the wounded, and in the light of a flashlight I examined the suffering men.

One Frenchman had had his ear pierced by a bullet. I congratulated him on being so lucky. Another man was lying unconscious on the floor with a bleeding wound and a large bruise on his forehead. The others had only minor wounds which needed no special attention. I dressed the wounds of the two Frenchmen as well as possible and noticed that the man on the floor only pretended to be unconscious, probably to enjoy his comfortable position. I asked the guards for water for the wounded, and surprisingly I got it at the next stop. It never reached the wounded, though, because the can with the precious fluid was snatched from my hands by some thirsty Frenchmen. I called them names in my best French!

The train reached the German border in the middle of the night. So at last I had come to this hateful country, but not as a laborer, not as a student, not as a prisoner of war as the Nazis had wanted me to, but as a political criminal and in the eyes of the

Nazis more dangerous and contemptible than the meanest trash of society.

It was snowing then, but the temperature inside the car was far above the freezing point. For once there was an abundance of food, although hardly anybody could eat the bread and the too salty sausage we had received upon our departure. Our thirst was agonizing, and this food made it more unbearable.

In early morning the train stopped at a German station. The door of our car was thrown open, and we were ordered to take off our shoes and socks, to leave them behind, and to come out on the platform. Marching barefoot in the cold winter air we watched the faces of the people in the train on the opposite side of the platform. German men and women and German soldiers showed clearly their satisfaction over the scene of our suffering. Wasn't this another triumph for the "Heil Hitler Kultur"?

The prisoners from our car were assembled into smaller groups and forced into other already overcrowded cattle cars where the inmates received us with loud grumbling. In one corner of my new prison lay the body of an elderly Frenchman. According to the French doctor, who was in this car from the beginning of the trip, the man had died of a perforated gastric ulcer. A few other Frenchmen had found a comfortable seat on his remains. At every station when the train stopped, we shouted through the bars of the small window to the guards on the platform asking them to remove the body. Finally when it was almost noon, the Germans complainingly took out the dead body.

Our thirst grew continually worse. Our tongues and palates were hard and dry. Several men began to lose their composure, and the first fights began among the prisoners. It would not be long until most of us would go crazy. Another night fell, and still I had not sat down for a single moment. My knees started to give way. Then at last I found a small spot where I could squat, and where I could breathe eagerly the cold and fresh stream of air that entered underneath the door.

In the darkness of the car I could not see a hand before my

eyes. The crying and scuffles went on uninterruptedly. Pandemonium reigned. Suddenly I felt two hands around my neck, and a voice in French snarled, "Get up, or I'll beat you to death; I want to sit here."

At random I gave him a blow with my fist. The grip around my neck lost its strength. Another blow and the man let go, falling upon some others whose cursing showed their anger. That one had already lost his senses.

We expected to be freighted either to the concentration camp of Buchenwald, near Weimar, or to that of Oranienburg, also known by its other name of Sachsenhausen, near Berlin. We figured this out by the cities we had passed the previous day. Frankfurt had been one of them, and the sight of that city had encouraged us as it lay in ruins, showing the work of Allied bombs.

I had never wanted to see the camp of Buchenwald. Far from that, I feared it tremendously. But now I hoped to be there soon, as it would at least mean the end of the horror in the cattle car. That night I, too, began to show the first signs of losing full control over my intellectual faculties and realized that the journey must soon be over or I would lose my senses completely. Yet, when I later heard stories about other transports, stories that told of deeds so inhuman and beastly that I could never repeat them, then I realized that our own transport had been one of the less horrible. The train stopped and then moved on again. "They are shunting the train," flashed through my mind. The end of one nightmare arrived; another one was about to start.

Suddenly the door of our car was flung open. A large gang of S.S. men armed with guns, sticks and whips and accompanied by furious, barking bloodhounds stood waiting for us to get out of the cars. We jumped down and tried to keep out of reach of the whips. We tore our bare feet open on the sharp stones which were covered with a thin layer of snow. Those of us who were not quick enough received a brutal beating or felt the sharp teeth of the dogs.

After two days and two nights in an overcrowded cattle car,

where men had almost become beasts in their struggle for survival, we were driven barefooted in the snow past the crematorium where already the cadavers of our own transport were being stacked. Our first intimate acquaintance with one of the most notorious products of the Nazi-Kultur was on that sixteenth day of December, 1943, at four o'clock in the morning.

"Right or wrong, my country," was the slogan of the concentration camp of Buchenwald where life had brought us. Shivering in the cold night I saw the word "Buchenwald" in letters of fire before my eyes. Buchenwald concentration camp! Was I to come out alive? Too often back in Holland had we heard of the crimes of this notorious place. My friends and I looked at each other. None of us said a word. We knew without speaking the others' thoughts.

But perhaps it would not be as horrible as the atrocious stories we had heard. Perhaps. Soon we would have first-hand information.

❧ *14* ❦

Buchenwald camp, which eventually became the grave for 51,000 human beings, had opened its gates in 1937, and the first to enter were prisoners from the Germans themselves. There were murderers, criminals, Jews, Gypsies, homosexuals, "asocials," Jehovah's Witnesses. The German Communists soon followed, and from the time Hitler started his all-out campaign, the great mass of political enemies from the occupied countries entered through the iron gates. All were thrown together, but in the systematic Nazi way and according to their methods of "divide-and-conquer," prisoners were separated into groups and given patches to sew on their trousers and coats. By these patches their crimes were known.

Those who were hostile to the Nazi rule because of political reasons, mostly Communists, wore a red triangle; those who were opposed because of religious motives, the Jehovah's Witnesses, wore a purple triangle. The criminals were divided into two groups: those who had committed one or several murders wore a green-colored triangle with a black "S" in it, while those who were merely burglars and thieves wore a plain green-colored triangle; both groups were generally known as the "greens." The Jews were compelled to wear a yellow star of David, the homosexuals a pink colored triangle and the "asocials," like the Gypsies, a black one.

All other nationalities wore a red-colored triangle with the first letter of the name of their fatherland inside. The Dutch prisoners, for instance, wore a red triangle with the initial "N." The only exceptions to this rule were the Jehovah's Witnesses, who, German or not, always wore a purple triangle. This religious sect had sent a personal letter to Hitler in which they had

prophesied by virtue of certain scripture texts that Nazi Germany
was doomed and that Hitler himself would die in its ruins. As
their understanding of the Bible also forbids them to kill other
human beings, they refused to join the armed forces and so had
been considered worthless and useless individuals only fit to join
the ranks of the political criminals in the concentration camps.
Was it superstition of the Nazis that in the latter and more
unfavorable years of the war they offered the members of this
religious sect their freedom if only they would recant their
prophecy? Not one Jehovah's Witness agreed to do so!

Of all those different groups, the criminals and the Communists played the most important role in Buchenwald's existence.
The criminals strictly speaking did not belong in a concentration
camp, but as most of them had to serve life sentences and as they,
like the Jews, the homosexuals and the asocials, were thought to
be utterly worthless and dangerous in the Third Reich, they had
been put away in these camps.

A concentration camp is a community in itself, and it was
only a logical sequence that a kind of government was formed
among the prisoners themselves. During the first years of
Buchenwald's existence, it had been the group of criminals, the
"greens," that had possessed the power. On rare occasions the
survivors of those years would tell me of the unspeakable terror
for all prisoners who did not wear a green triangle. I could not be
thankful enough that I had not arrived a few years earlier. I could
easily fill many pages with almost unbelievable horror stories,
compared to which the stories of Edgar Allan Poe could be used
as lullabies; but as I have them, fortunately, only from hearsay, I
have told solely what I myself know to be true.

With the infiltration of the political prisoners into the camp,
a revolution could not be avoided, and several months before my
arrival the leading, powerful criminals had been murdered one
night by the Communists who, from then on, had occupied all the
important positions. Whereas the criminals had been simply out
for their own individual welfare, murdering and killing indis-
criminately, and showing little group cohesiveness, it had not

been too difficult for the more than three hundred German Communists who always worked closely together to infiltrate gradually among them and force them one by one out of their influential positions. The whole coup had been deliberately planned and was crowned with success when the last criminals had been killed. Buchenwald had become a Red center in the heart of Nazi Germany! Although the Communists had ultimately more power over their fellow prisoners than the S.S. did, the Nazis did not object as long as their commands were obeyed, and as long as the prisoners helped them in their extermination plans by mutual discord, dissension, and murder.

Yes, even one S.S. officer, Dr. Hoven, seemed to have been a partisan of the Communist party, helping them considerably in killing the criminals by injections of phenol into the heart. It had always struck me that on the rare occasions when a Communist spoke of this officer, there was a certain respect in his voice. When I saw Dr. Hoven for the first and last time a few days before our liberation in the company of the German Communists, he seemed to get along quite well with them. So the Communists, mainly German, though also those of other nationalities, had the power of life and death over all the other inmates of the camp. It was they who organized a deadly terror within the Nazi terror; it was they who were the main characters of a hideous story of treachery by prisoners against prisoners.

It might be called strange that the German Communists played a much more important role in the politics of the camp than the Russian prisoners did. But this is only so for those who live under the impression that "Russian" is synonymous with "Communist." They who know that only three percent of the Russian population are members of the Communist party will readily see that among the Russian prisoners not many Communists were to be expected.

The Russians formed a larger contingent than any of the other Slavic nations in Buchenwald. Of these Russians, some were prisoners of war and some, the majority, were civilians. The Russian soldiers arrived regularly in huge and numerous transports. They were led into the S.S. sound-proof riding school and riddled with machine gun bullets. The men who escaped being shot in this mass murder were put in separate blocks. Though these Russians were distinguished by not having to wear camp numbers, they were treated exactly like the other prisoners. This prisoner of war group always kept to itself, and since in it were high officials, including several colonels, military discipline was well-maintained.

In general, I liked the Russians very much. With a few kind words of interest, with some extra food, they easily became one's most devoted friends. Those young boys who had known so little of a real home — products of the State as many were — still had a soul that longed for kindness and affability. Though many of the young Russians appeared to have been educated in complete ignorance of religion and of a God, they certainly could not be called Communists. Rather should they be considered victims of the Communist regime that forbade all forms of religious worship in their homeland.

It was a matter of sentiment that I liked them, because as they spoke little of any language but their own it was practically impossible to discuss any serious matters. But shouldn't we at times listen more to the voice of our emotions than to the voice of our reason and intellect? I had personal enemies among my fellow prisoners of many nationalities, even among my own countrymen. But I cannot remember that there was one Russian who ever wished me misfortune or death. I firmly believe that the Russian people, once freed from their oppressors, the Communist clique, will become a great asset not only to democracy but also to religion. As Germany was freed from its oppressor Nazism, so also one day will Russia be liberated from its Communist terror.

❧ *15* ❧

We had nothing but our bodies and souls after we had gone through the "disinfection building" that morning of our arrival. Every hair on our head and body had been shaved off in order to be rid of lice. After a shower followed by a spray with a disinfecting material we were given beggar's clothes and wooden shoes to replace our own clothes, which had been taken from us together with our other belongings. What a sight we were! The Dutchmen walked as poorly and as painfully on their national wooden shoes as the Frenchmen. I thought of the only time in my life that I had ever worn wooden shoes — it had been at the photographer's when the whole family had posed for a "real Dutch picture."

My first acquaintance with a fellow prisoner proved later to be extremely fortunate. It was with Professor Telders, professor of law at the University of Leiden in Holland. He had been in Buchenwald for a long time, and he knew most of the ropes and tricks of getting along in this place of intrigue and death. He had a job with the "Politisch Abteilung," or "Political Bureau," which was one of the departments in the camp run entirely by the prisoners themselves, but still under the direct supervision of the S.S. The professor questioned all the new arrivals about their personal history. He filled in cards for each prisoner, and these cards were kept on file in the camp.

When I was giving the professor my personal history, I told him that I had been a medical student for the past five years though I did not yet have my degree. He advised me at once to pretend to be a fully qualified physician. I objected to doing that as I was afraid I could not live up to the responsibilities and duties of such a status. Even the experience of the last weeks had not yet deadened all feelings of civilized life and thinking; I still had many things to learn in this new life!

But the professor had already written down "doctor" on my record, and he told me that I soon would find out for myself that this title was justified. Indeed, it was not long before I realized that the physicians in the hospital had never studied medicine nor were interested in it until they found out that a job in the camp hospital had material advantages. These prisoner-"physicians" even competed with the S.S. in their disgraceful and devilish practices, to the detriment of their patients. So later when I found myself working with bicycle repairmen, barbers, and political agitators taking care of the sick, I felt no qualms about my pretended title.

I spent the required four weeks in the quarantine camp, which was a separate part of the compound. Then, as the only Dutchman of our transport, I was selected to go with 499 Frenchmen to "Dora," one of the worst outside commandos of Buchenwald, where monthly about a thousand prisoners died of starvation and exhaustion, if not plain murder, on the construction of the V-bomb. But the advice of Professor Telders was to save me from a certain death. When we had a "medical examination" by an S.S. officer, who did nothing but collect the cards we had been given and on which were only our political records, I stood before S.S. Hauptsturmfuehrer, Dr. Schieldlausky, who seemed to be interested in the information on my card.

"Are you a doctor?" he asked me.

"Yes," I answered, but did not add as was compulsory, his title of Hauptsturmfuehrer, as I could not think of anything but "general," and that title seemed rather improbable. Until the day of liberation I never was able, in spite of the daily presence of so many S.S. officers, to make any distinction in their uniform badges except that of high or low.

So I said "yes" and got away with it.

"Have you already your doctor's degree?" he questioned.

"Yes."

"Have you practiced already in Holland?"

Again I assented without batting an eyelid even though I realized that my hairless head did not help any to make my already youngish-looking face appear older. But my life depended on my self-assurance; one moment of uncertainty on my part, and my record card would be put with those of the 499 Frenchmen who, young or old, sick or healthy, invalid or not, had been approved in twenty minutes to live another six weeks, the average lifetime in the hell of "Dora." The Hauptsturmfuehrer put a mark on my card and told me that I was not to go on the transport. My guardian angel was still by my side!

It appeared that a new order from Berlin had been received recently that all doctors, who until then had not been allowed to work in the hospital, were to give their attention to the sick. These trained men had formerly been sent to slave in the stone quarry, or they had been put on a transport.

But why this change of attitude toward the doctors? Was Berlin seeing the turn for the worse in their campaign and seeing the approach of the day of reckoning? Or was it because too many slave laborers were dying? I cannot believe the last, considering the startling number of prisoners that entered after me. My prison number was 38263, and sixteen months later the 150,000th prisoner had entered through prison gates. The prison number of those who had died was always used again, and sometimes used two or three times in succession. It could be safely figured that approximately 8,000 prisoners a month were absorbed by this concentration camp alone.

The next day I was put to work as a nurse in the major section of the camp hospital. It seemed that the prisoners who under the S.S. were in charge of the hospital had not fallen for my pretended title. But I soon discovered that the position of nurse had greater material advantages than that of doctor. The most important of these was to have a bed of my own. At the same time, I was able to examine and to treat the patients according to my own opinion, for the diagnosis and advice for treatment of the official "doctor" was usually inadequate.

I was appointed as an assistant nurse in a 40-bed tuberculosis ward. My superior nurse was a German criminal condemned to prison for murder! In spite of the fact that the criminal group had lost all their power in the camp not long before when the Communist prisoners had taken control, this man had been able to get this greatly desired job as nurse because, he let it be known, he had "connections" with one of the S.S. officers. The intrigues in the camp appeared rather complicated to me, but experience teaches fools.

During the first weeks of my new job, I was glad not to have to carry the responsibilities of a doctor, for due to the starvation in the French prisons, aggravated by the mental tortures during the transport to Buchenwald, I had lost most of my memory. I could not remember the names of my friends in Holland, nor names of places I had been, but worst of all it was as if I had never studied medicine before. I vaguely remembered that tuberculosis was some unpleasant disease, but I had to be told that I should watch out for being infected and that I should regularly wash my hands in Lysol. When someone talked about a patient having pneumonia, I was unable to understand what this meant. In short I lived like a robot during that period. I was completely passive, and I had not the slightest interest for my patients whom I could not understand. But fortunately my memory gradually returned and my mind cleared as I grew stronger with the help of the larger amounts of food I was given in the hospital.

I will never forget that first night in the hospital when again I had a bed with a mattress well-filled with straw. I even had sheets, blankets and a pillow. All that night I was plagued by terrible nightmares; every other moment I jumped out of bed, covered with perspiration. Finally I fell into an exhausting sleep from which I was soon awakened to start the daily work. After these wild dreams, I lived that day in another nightmare under my criminal supervisor. His prime interest was his privileged position and the material benefits that came with it. That he had to distribute medicine to the sick, he did merely to keep his job. He called me the vilest names, blamed me for every mistake, and gave me the dirtiest jobs. He kept me working hours into the night. At the time, I desperately needed rest in order to regain my moral strength so as not to lose my courage. The following day I refused to return to my bed when I had a temperature of 104 degrees and a seriously inflamed throat. I was so afraid the German criminal would take this opportunity to have me lose this job that I kept working. Already I began to suspect and distrust my fellow prisoners.

About ten days after I had been working in the tuberculosis ward, I suddenly became furious at the nagging of the criminal nurse even though I did not yet fully realize how dangerous for me could be his attempts to make me appear ridiculous and stupid in front of the others. When he told me for the hundredth time that I was no good and that I would never be able to take charge of a ward myself, I lost my patience and replied that he could stay in bed the next day and that I would do all the work myself; also that I would show him how it ought to be done. A scornful laugh was my answer. That same afternoon when I was taking the temperatures, the "Kapo"[1] of the hospital entered the ward shouting, "Say, Baars, have you learned enough here to take charge of a ward yourself?"

"Certainly," I replied quickly. Here was my opportunity to be transferred to another place. The huge eyes of the surprised criminal were satisfying to watch, and before he could make any remark to interfere, I was ordered at once to the other ward.

What a relief to be away from that criminal! But I was ignorant, of course, of the more serious dangers that threatened me in my new position as nurse of a scarlet fever ward. I was grateful that the previous nurse here, a German Communist who had been imprisoned for nine years, had caught scarlet fever, and I wished him a few months of hospitalization. My wish materialized, for he developed one complication after another — kidney infection, middle ear infection, pleurisy, and rheumatic fever.

I had not been many days in my new ward when one day I received orders that all the patients had to be evacuated. Those who had almost finished their time of quarantine were returned to their barracks in the camp, the others were found beds in other

[1] Prisoner in charge of a certain department in the camp.

wards in the hospital. What was the meaning of this change in routine? The only thing I could find out was that a very important person would be admitted to my ward. He was not to come in contact with the prisoners, and I was told that I had to be very careful in my conversation with him if I did not want to endanger my life. That this person was to arrive from the prison jail made the situation more of a mystery.

That night after roll call a short, tremendously fat, pajama-clad man came into my empty, clean ward, where one of the thirteen beds had been removed to make more room. I could hardly keep from smiling at this clownish-looking figure, but Dr. M., a Czech and the chief doctor of our barrack, jumped up and seriously greeted him. The poor doctor, who had become very nervous waiting for the important patient, immediately examined him. A slight inflammation of the throat was the diagnosis!

The doctor left, and I was alone with the new patient. It was impossible to ignore him, so I decided to get some information. He was willing to talk, and he explained that he was an S.S. officer! At that bit of unexpected news, I became apprehensive; what was I mixed up in now?

The man went on talking. His name was Johan Galbavi, Edler von Wohlerstal, something of the equivalent of "nobleman of Wohlerstal." He was an Austrian by birth, and his mother had been lady-in-waiting at the court of the Austrian Emperor in Vienna. The man claimed that he spoke fourteen languages — all the Slavic languages, French, English, Turkish and Arabic. I thought he was bragging, but I found out later that it was all true. When he talked with my "kalfactor" — the boy who cleaned the room — the latter had said he was a Russian. I had to admit to the nobleman he was correct when he told me that the boy had lied and that he was a Ukrainian.

I asked my patient why he could not be treated in the S.S. hospital, upon which he replied that he had many enemies among the S.S., and that his life would not be safe in their hospital.

During the next few days, I learned that the man had been jailed for embezzlement as chief of the S.S. canteen. But this

sounded suspicious, especially when I found out from other
prisoners, who had been in Buchenwald since its opening in 1937,
that they thought the nobleman was a spy, and that he had come
here to investigate the frauds in the hospital during the time of
S.S. Hauptsturmfuehrer Dr. Hoven's command. Dr. Hoven himself was now spending his days in idleness in the prison of
Weimar for his crimes.

Intrigues among the S.S. themselves were as prevalent as
among the prisoners. Little wonder. Any job as S.S. guard, especially the more important ones as that of Commander of the
camp, were highly profitable. A great fortune could be made by
robbing the prisoners when they entered the camp, and by using
them as slave labor.

S.S. Commander Koch was the most accomplished of in-
triguers, but he became too wealthy and too careless and was
finally hung on a hook till he died in the cellar of the crematorium
by his own jealous S.S. men. Koch had a beautiful house built by
the prisoners; he had furniture manufactured by the skilled slave
laborers; he had portraits of his whole family done by an artist
prisoner; he had valuables worth five million dollars which were
taken from the new arrivals. So it was likely that his friends would
become jealous and wish him dead. Now his successor enjoyed
the same prosperity.

His wife, the notorious Ilse Koch, had been his "faithful"
companion, though at the same time she had much more original
ideas. She had a special preference for prisoners with tattoos, who
then went the way of all flesh except for their skin, which went the
way of cozy lamp-shades in Frau Koch's boudoir and the way of
purses and wallets with which she became extremely popular
among all her girlfriends! This new expression of "art," developed in the twentieth century, marked the summit of Nazi
Kultur!

The nobleman of Austrian blood stayed in my ward for
forty-five days after his angina had been cured. This made it all
the more probable that he was here on a special mission. Though
I had been instructed to forbid all contact between him and the

prisoners, I soon gave up trying as I had absolutely no authority over him. His winning manner, his undeniable knowledge of human character, and his astounding linguistic abilities easily acquainted him with everybody he met. He even broke down the reserve of those who were convinced that he was a dangerous character, and who were always on the alert to avoid speaking about anything that might be perilous to their lives.

Every day the "honored" patient received special food from the S.S. kitchen, and he usually gave me part of it. Naturally I enjoyed the change from the daily ration of bread and soup. The times he was very hungry, he would want some of my soup, but I had to taste it first to assure him that it had not been poisoned. He would say to me: "If anything happens to me while I am in your ward, you will be killed. So will that doctor and the Kapo." That's a pleasant thought to go to bed with, I said to myself.

The S.S. officer's conscience obviously gave him a lot of trouble. Every morning when I awakened him, he would jump upright with fear and suspicion in his eyes to fall back onto his pillow relieved to see that it was only I.

One day I woke him to give him an injection for a few pimples that were caused, in my opinion, by too much fat in his diet. After he had made his usual jump, I said, "I must give you an injection of calcium. It is Hauptsturmfuehrer Dr. Rogge's order."

"No, no," he shouted, "you want to kill me. I won't have it!"

"Listen," I told him, "I wouldn't kill you. You said yourself that if anything happens to you I shall die, too. Here, see the label." I showed him the label on the ampule. He had no more objections. The fool! He had no proof that the syringe contained the same solution as the ampule that I held out to him. Perhaps, though, he realized that I would not risk my own head by killing him.

One morning my patient was summoned to report to the Hauptsturmfuehrer in his office, but he asked me to tell him that he could not come as he had slept badly and wanted to stay in bed. I delivered the message and returned to the ward. Within a few minutes the door was flung open and Dr. Rogge rushed in, red with fury. He called the nobleman all the bad names he could think of, and they were many, while the nobleman himself sat up in bed almost crying, offering his excuses and promising to go at once to the office. He was punished by having to shovel snow on the hospital grounds for the next few days. This gave him a good opportunity to talk to everyone, and to get information, if that was what he was after.

Experienced prisoners learned that the wisest behavior in the camp was to pretend to know nothing. No one was ever told about irregular or unofficial happenings. You had to use your eyes and keep to yourself what you saw, for knowing something could be very dangerous. Playing dumb was playing safe! Why? Because you could never know to what kind of person you were talking, or on whose side that person was, or what powers he might have. By telling someone something interesting or unusual, you might give yourself away as being an enemy — and enemies were eliminated ruthlessly. Especially men like me who were unimportant, who had no influence, and who were the declared enemies of the powerful, reigning, Communist group among the prisoners. So everyone tried to play dumb with the nobleman. From the first day on, he tried to get me into debates over Holland and our Queen, or he tried to learn more about my personal background. But I avoided carefully all slippery ground, as it might be disastrous if he learned about my underground activities. I could never make out whether or not he really was in disgrace with the Nazis and so more inclined to share the prisoners' feelings of hatred for the Nazi philosophy. If he was not, he and the S.S. certainly played their roles extremely well. We were glad to see him leave the hospital. I doubted if he had been successful in his mission.

The main thing was that I had come through the affair unscathed. It had been an interesting experience: a prisoner of the S.S. nursing an S.S. officer himself!

❧ *16* ❦

The Scandinavian countries were represented in Buchenwald by large groups of Norwegians and Danes. In January, 1944, five hundred healthy, energetic Norwegian students from the University of Oslo were brought to our camp. These men had been arrested and imprisoned because they had refused to work for the Nazi occupier. They were kept away from the other prisoners and did not live by the usual hard camp rules. The S.S. had given them special privileges — they did not have to have their heads shaved, they ate the good food from the S.S. kitchen, and they did not have to work.

In spite of the fact that they were better off than the rest of us, we felt no envy because we all liked and respected these fine young men for their good spirits and brave attitude. Perhaps, too, we were suspicious that such good treatment was but a fattening for the kill. And so it was. Six months later the strong, well-fed Norwegians were sent to an S.S. training camp in Germany to be made into German soldiers. But the Norwegian students, who would not work for the Nazi war machine, would certainly not fight against the Allies and against freedom. Even after the S.S. had urged them first with promises and then with threats, the students had refused to join the "glorious" German army. They ripped all the distinguishing marks of the S.S. from the uniforms they had been given. Even the belt with the "Gott mit uns" buckle they had thrown away and replaced with a piece of rope.

The S.S. Commander was in despair. He had promised his superiors to deliver these young men ready for the "Great German Drive" at the front. The students, then ordered back to the concentration camp, marched ten days and nights without food or shelter. One night they were exposed to the terrible R.A.F.

103

bombing of Freiburg, where all but one of them miraculously survived. And so they returned to Buchenwald exhausted, starved, at the end of their physical strength, but with even more courage in their hearts than when they had left. They had fought a good fight against their enemy, they knew what they believed in, and they stood by that belief in the face of death. No wonder we prisoners respected and admired them! And the more we learned of their courage, the more we were strengthened in our own determination to be steadfast and not overcome by fear.

In spite of the moral defeat the S.S. had suffered, the Norwegians on their return to camp still were not treated as common prisoners, but were given the privileges they had had before. As this time they did not have a hospital ward of their own, I was able to know them better when six of them were sent to my scarlet fever ward for hospitalization. It was pleasant for me to talk to and enjoy fellow students, whose interests were more akin to mine than those of most of the men I nursed in the camp.

One day a Norwegian, Tor Vangberg, a fair-haired, handsome young man, came to my ward seriously ill with sepsis, a general blood poisoning. Tor was going to die — it was certain. Nonetheless, I was going to do all I could to save him — in spite of the lack of medicine. I stayed with him constantly, I stole drugs to give him, and I sought help from a Norwegian doctor. The Russian doctor, Sulikov, prescribed a treatment that would have meant immediate death to my patient — naturally I ignored it. But after three days Tor died anyway. All my energy and care had gone only to postpone the hour of his death and to prolong his struggling.

Why had I tried the impossible? Early in my imprisonment I had seen that because of the lack of adequate medicine and food, men — even young men — died of illnesses that under normal circumstances were not serious. I had forced myself to develop a hardness of heart and indifference in the face of unavoidable death. But Tor had shown what so many of the other patients had lacked — the determination to fight to the last breath with our only powerful medicine here — a firm trust in God and His goodness. What else could I have done but help him as well as I could? And in this struggle against death, my feelings of sympathy and compassion had taken too great a part, because without these feelings this struggle cannot be complete. And so as I sat beside the dying Norwegian, my indifference softened and the sympathetic human feelings that I tried so hard to suppress overwhelmed me in a cruel way. Why had this young man to die? Why was there so much misery and suffering? I wept and I was ashamed of my tears. Had I not seen misery enough that by now I should be immune to it? No more, I decided, would I try to do the impossible. No more would I try to avoid a certain death. Only the possible would I do — to offer a kind word to the miserable and a piece of bread to the hungry.

It was only when I realized anew that this misery and suffering were not willed by God, but merely tolerated and used as the instruments in His hands toward a goal that I in that moment of depression could not understand — it was only then that I was able to overcome this moral collapse.

It was also with the help of the Norwegians, whom I often visited back in their own barrack, that I was able to get back my old courage. Their zeal and spirit was so strong that I eagerly sought their company and intelligent conversation. I visited them on one condition — that they give me none of their food which they received frequently from Sweden and Norway. Their barrack was always surrounded by beggars, so I did not want my friends to think that I, too, came for material presents, rather than for their own selves.

But too soon they were to leave Buchenwald. I will always remember their farewell. I felt so ashamed when they came to bring me seven large food parcels they had collected among them. Their friendship alone was worth more to me than I could ever repay. The interest and sympathy that all the prisoners expressed at the departure of these students for the camp of Neuengamme proved how much they were liked and esteemed. If there was any group in Buchenwald that deserved to escape the claws of the Nazis, it was that of the Norwegian students!

We eagerly awaited the arrival of the two thousand Danish police from Copenhagen, as we had found such excellent comrades in their Nordic brothers, the Norwegians. But our expectations had been too high, and there were few of us who regretted their leaving Buchenwald after their several months' stay in 1944, when they were returned to Denmark through the intervention of the Danish Red Cross.

Several epidemics had broken out among these seemingly vigorous Danes almost as soon as they had arrived in camp. Here in the contagious wards, I was in close contact with many of them. Scarlet fever raged frightfully, attacking five hundred men in one week. The combined number of cases of erysipelas, pneumonia, and the dreaded phlegmons[1] reached almost a thousand. Many Danes suffering from erysipelas developed toxic psychoses. Death took many of them. I believe that in relation to their number, their excellent nutrition, and their short stay in camp compared to the rest of the prisoners, their deaths surpassed those of any other group.

Every week each Danish prisoner received packages of food and clothing from the Red Cross. They hardly needed to eat camp food or wear the prisoner uniforms. Soon the less privileged prisoners began to dislike their new comrades, the Danes, for they never shared their bounty with anyone. It was a sensitive point, this sharing, in a community like a prison camp.

The men from Copenhagen had come from a country that in spite of four years of war still flowed with milk and honey. Most of them had never eaten black bread and refused to eat this most precious part of our daily rations. Naturally, I never forced them to eat it, as there were enough hungry mouths for whom an extra portion of black bread was manna from heaven.

Their little country had capitulated without any struggle and had never experienced the hardships of war. It had not been plundered of its riches like the other overpowered countries. No wonder that, suddenly transplanted to such an amorally and

---

[1] Tumors caused by inflammations.

physically unhealthy place as Buchenwald, they became the victims of their own conduct during the time of occupation.

The Danes were unconcerned about the suffering of others, and even among themselves did not practice charity. One evening an elderly policeman suffering with a huge phlegmon of the breast came to my ward. After Hermann, the Kapo, had seen him, he forbade me to give the patient any of our rare prontosil tablets, as he considered recovery hopeless. The Dane was doomed to die! I went to talk to the patient to see if I could be of any spiritual help to him in his last days, and to find out if he wanted to give me any special messages for his relatives. He told me how, long ago, he, too, had studied to become a doctor, but that he had had to give up his studies when his father died. He then had to earn his living as a policeman. He was happily married and had five children, one of whom was already a doctor and another an engineer.

I became more and more uneasy during our heart-to-heart talk, knowing that a few minutes before his fate had been decided upon. Was there nothing I could do? I examined the man carefully and decided to start him on a prontosil cure in spite of Hermann's order to the contrary. Prontosil had by that time become so scarce that only the younger, most vigorous and least sick of the patients were given the drug, as they would have the greatest possibility of responding well to the treatment. The more progressive and serious cases who would need larger doses were refused the prontosil. I explained the whole situation to the Danish policeman and impressed on him that he should tell no one about my giving him this medicine.

In a few weeks the phlegmon had disappeared, even without an incision and drainage of pus. I almost began to doubt the correctness of the diagnosis, he had responded so well. Then the cured patient left my ward without a single word of gratitude. He was loaded down with food parcels which he had shared with no one in the ward. After his departure, Roland found a piece of moldy cheese and a pound of completely spoiled butter hidden in his mattress. Some people certainly knew well the value of their own life. A few days later I had another elderly Danish police officer in my ward. He had developed sepsis following scarlet fever. Soon the man was near death. It surprised me that none of his countrymen paid any attention to him. I did not want to interfere, but I could see that the man needed some kind words. He could talk only a little German with me, and that language he spoke with great difficulty. The morning after he died, a Danish police major asked me what the man had died of.

"Why are you so curious?" I asked.

"I have known him for twenty years. He was my good friend," he answered indifferently. I was appalled at his lack of human sympathy and kindness, which his countryman had needed so much.

Such people we could not use in Buchenwald, and we rejoiced when they were returned to Denmark. After all, they had been arrested by the Germans more as a matter of authority and not because they had committed any acts directly hostile to the German occupation.

❧ *17* ❧

"God you do not need any longer in Buchenwald!" With these words the Communist prisoner, upon my arrival in the camp, had torn my rosary to pieces and trampled the remnants under his feet. Religion, at least all outward signs pertaining to it, was non-existent in this concentration camp. But the spirit of religion did exist, for it cannot be killed, anywhere, not even in the hell of Buchenwald, for those who are in need of God, for those who realize that life is God and that God is life.

It was among the French prisoners that I found a man who would enable me to live my religion in its fullest glory. There were many thousands of Frenchmen at Buchenwald, and as a group they were scorned and despised. The word "Francais" — with the accent on the first syllable — had originally been intended as an invective for the French only, but later it had become an abusive word for everybody, French or not. How contemptuously the Slavic prisoners pronounced this word! Like the Belgians and the Dutch, the French represented a menace to the German Communists because of their Western outlook, but they hated the French because of the historical enmity between the two nations, Germany and France, and now they despised them more because of France's humiliating defeat in the summer of 1940. As the Germans often said, "If France had only been strong enough and successful in their resistance to Hitler's invading armies, the war would have been over much sooner."

A Frenchman was at a disadvantage in Buchenwald because of his nationality. The labor office, the key position of the powerful German Communists, made up the transports and gave the French prisoner every priority for shipment to the dreaded death commandos. The "Dora" camp, the most fatal of these, took monthly more than a thousand dead — and most of these were Frenchmen! Though personally I had had pleasant experiences in France, this sympathy nevertheless diminished when I got to know the Frenchmen in difficult and trying circumstances. In time of need, one learns to know one's friends!

The trip from Compiegne to Buchenwald in the cattle cars had already given me much food for thought about the character of the French. Later on I had enough opportunities to see how degenerate most of the Frenchmen were, especially the younger ones who mainly through lack of moral strength fell victims to hardships which only by a firm belief in God and in oneself could be conquered.

Once on the battlefields of World War I, now in the concentration camps of World War II, France paid its price for taking the lead in one of the most successful campaigns in modern history some one hundred and twenty five years earlier: the campaign of birth control. Successful their campaign had been, because birth control appeals so much to the selfish element in every human being. It eliminates the responsibilities and duties of love, it decries the consequence of romance, and it educates young people in their own selfish interest and in the indulgence of their selfish pleasures. France, by destroying the morality of its youth, had led the way to the destruction of its own existence; it had removed in its children the backbone of perseverance against evil. They had nobody to blame but themselves, not even their executioners, the Communists, who were only supporting Malthus' theory that the mad, rabbit-like multiplication of the members of the human race would cause a disastrous exhaustion of the world's food supply.

There were several good men among the French prisoners, but one man I knew personally, who stood out through his shining example of Christian life, Père George, a Catholic priest from Nancy in France. Bernard Norman, my good friend since the prison days at Toulouse, introduced me to him one day. It was a privilege for which I cannot be grateful enough. This good priest was a help to hundreds of desolate prisoners. Every evening one could see him walk in front of his barrack in the mud, now with one, now with another prisoner, who had come to him to confess his sins and to receive absolution. Never in my life shall I forget that evening just before Easter 1944, when for the first time in many months I had gone to Father George for confession. As the weather was too bad, we had to stay inside the barrack, and there, among the hundreds of prisoners whose turmoil filled the air, he heard my sins. All the inmates of the barrack were French, so Père George and I spoke German to prevent the nearest persons from overhearing us, because what we did was a crime in the eyes of our virtual masters, the Communists.

Christmas 1943 had been such an unspeakably sad day for my friends and me in the filthy, crowded quarters of the quarantine camp, as we tried not to hear the cabaret songs of a French crooner amusing his countrymen. Easter 1944 was a day never to forget. I received Holy Communion from the hands of Père George!

There in the midst of the Communist hell of Buchenwald, with not even the privacy the Christians in the Roman catacombs were able to enjoy, God came to me in the form of bread. From that day on I was able to receive Holy Communion every morning as Père George gave me regularly one or more consecrated Hosts that I was able to carry with me every day and night.

Yes, I know I was totally unworthy to carry the Holy Host with me, even more so to touch it with my hands, but it was the only possible way of receiving Him whom I needed so badly in my misfortune. It was His continuous presence and His grace that carried me unharmed through all the dangers of the long hours of my captivity. What this precious gift from Père George had meant to me I cannot possibly describe. God does not leave His children when they are in need. And He knows only too well which of them, like me, need His help the most.

I had been able to give Holy Communion to a few of my patients in their last hours, but they were all too few. The overcrowded wards made this extremely dangerous, and only when I was sure that the patients in the adjoining beds would not be able to understand one language or the other, could I instruct the dying man so that our Sacred Secret would not be endangered.

Though I do not know what the Communists or the S.S. would have done if they had found out about these religious activities, it was not the fear of their eventual reprisals that made us guard our actions with the utmost secrecy, but the fear that we Catholics would be deprived of the only solace that made our existence tolerable. But they never did find out. It was the secret story of the wheel of religion within the wheel of Communism within the wheel of Nazism. The final secret of how the hosts came to Father George I never learned, as I never wanted to ask him about it. My knowledge could only have endangered him and others.

The day he and all the other Catholic priests were transferred to the concentration camp at Dachau near Munich was a sorrowful one, but he had taught us how to live, and he had given us the means of continuing his blessed work.

Kissing me on both cheeks when we parted, Père George blessed me. For once I was not ashamed of the tears in my eyes.

❧ *18* ❧

The first of June I was transferred to the quarantine camp hospital, which consisted of two wooden barracks. Certainly this change was no promotion, but instead a clear indication of the Communists' dislike for me. The Czech nurses and doctors who had bedeviled me those months in the scarlet fever ward had also succeeded in bringing my name into disrepute. My being a Catholic, an intellectual, and the son of a capitalist did not add to my popularity in this Communist stronghold. But they would not get me without a struggle, for I fully intended to fight back, although not under false pretenses, as so many prisoners were, by taking any but an anti-Communist stand.

My new barrack was divided into two wards. Ward number nine was for the severest cases of lung tuberculosis. From this ward the patient usually went to the crematorium. The barrack had been a disgustingly filthy place until first a Dutchman and then a German had been put in charge. Both of these men were good organizers. "To organize" in camp slang was the euphemistic expression for "to steal." Such stealing was accomplished through a long chain of contacts. The nurses traded the bread of the dying tuberculosis patients for wood, mattresses and straw, things needed to make the ward a better place for the sick. The prisoners who worked in the S.S. commandos and had access to supplies had no scruples about stealing and selling anything they could.

My ward was number eight, where all the sick among the new arrivals in the quarantine camp were put. Although there were only sixty beds, we averaged approximately a hundred patients. We accommodated them the best we could by pushing two beds together and using them for three men. Every disease was here: pneumonia, tuberculosis, pleurisy, phlegmons, dysentery, meningitis, typhoid, and of course starvation. Attempts were made to transfer all the highly contagious diseases to special wards; however, tuberculosis was so prevalent that only the near-death cases were admitted to ward nine.

The nurse and his "kalfactor" were Polish and as a logical sequence, so were the majority of the patients. But as long as there were no Czechs to harass me as before, I had no complaints. On the contrary, I was eager to know these Poles better, especially the nurse, Leo, who had a good reputation in caring for his patients. He was said to work hard day and night doing as much as he could for them. Leo had been in the camp more than four years, and was now the only survivor of his transport of one thousand men from Poland. He had begun his imprisonment by working in the quarry which was at that time compulsory for all newcomers, during those first years of Buchenwald's notoriety. I certainly did not envy him his time there. I remembered only too well the few days I put in working in the quarry when I was in the quarantine camp. The wooden shoes would stick deep in the soft clay, and it was only with the utmost difficulty and pain that we could free them and plod on again. The boulders we had to carry weighed us down so that each step required a tremendous effort to pull our feet from the oozing mud. One day, my birthday, I had decided to celebrate by carrying the smallest stone I could find. I was half-way up the muddy hill when a prisoner foreman discovered my stratagem and knocked the stone off my shoulder. My "present" all but disappeared in the mud at my feet. Harshly the foreman ordered me back down to return with two heavy stones. I shall never forget that sad birthday party! But Leo had managed to work himself up and save his life by getting a job as a barber. Gradually he made influential friends, and now he himself was important and did not have much difficulty in getting the job of nurse in the hospital. I liked him immediately, for he had a great interest in his patients and had a comparatively good understanding of medicine in general. Eagerly he studied all the medical books available, and together we would translate them from Latin and French into German.

After being in the ward a few days, I noticed the friction between Leo and Alex, a young Russian who was the official doctor for our ward. True to history, Russia and Poland could not get along peacefully with each other. Alex's knowledge of doctoring was very slight, and I suspected that he had only been a first year medical student. Most of his cases he diagnosed as wet pleurisy, and these patients were lined up in a row to be punctured in the chest with a long but seldom sterile needle. No wonder we had so many collapsed lungs!

Leo and Alex had an unofficial agreement between them that Leo would attend all the Polish patients and Alex the Russian ones. Each man tried his best to admit as many of his own countrymen as possible to the hospital, thus saving them from the rigors of the quarantine camp. Alex, according to Leo, seemed to take advantage of this agreement. He kept his patients an extra length of time in bed and did his best to get the Polish patients discharged at the earliest possible moment.

But Leo was not going to let Alex get the better of him, and in order to be in a stronger position against the Russian and his followers, he tried to get my sympathy. Though I did like Alex in spite of his too liberal handling of my precious tobacco, I could not admire his professional activities. He blundered too much in diagnosis as well as in therapy. He paid too little attention to the well-being of his patients. In the mornings, after having raced along the patients' beds with a cigarette in his mouth, occasionally looking at the temperature lists I made twice a day, he would leave all the work to be done by Leo and me. So I took Leo's side, even though I had come to realize that it made little or no difference which man I favored, the one interested in his patients or the one who neglected them. The pitiful lack of medicine made cures almost impossible. But nevertheless, if everyone did his work well, the condition of the patients could be improved.

One day Leo went to the Kapo, the chief of the quarantine hospital, and asked his help to get Alex out of the ward. They planned that the next morning Hermann, the Kapo, would make his daily checkup earlier than usual, and thus surprise Alex, who often slept late. This would be sufficient reason to fire him, since his shortcomings frequently endangered the patients. But my position in the hospital and camp was already too precarious for me to intervene, and besides, I did not want to become involved in any intrigues. It was trouble enough to protect myself against those of others. Leo, who was a convinced Communist, was now very powerful in the camp, and it would be of no avail to go against him.

Two days later Alex was dismissed, but not through the original scheme. Alex had spoiled that by rising earlier than usual that morning. However, another reason was soon trumped up, and Alex left the camp on a transport as a doctor to one of Buchenwald's commandos.

One evening soon after this incident, Leo and I were walking through the ward after examining some newly admitted patients. Gradually our conversation became more personal. We discussed the pros and cons of Communism and then talked about medicine. I was much interested in hearing an absolute layman's opinion on this field of science. Surprisingly, Leo had a remarkable insight into the problems of medicine in general, although he was a barber who had never before studied a medical book. He confessed that he was very eager to take up the study of medicine if he should survive his imprisonment.

"Since Poland will be utterly impoverished after the war, how do you expect to get the money for your education?" I asked him.

"I hope to make sufficient money from a discovery that I have made here," he answered.

This sounded interesting. "What kind of discovery?"

He said simply, "Quite by accident I found a cure for tuberculosis." I must have looked completely dumbfounded, for he began to laugh.

"Leo, to find a cure for one of man's most terrible scourges! That's fantastic, too fantastic!" I sputtered.

Koert's mother Constance Baars-deGroot with (left to right) Koert, Walter Jr.,
Marie-José.

April 1928 — The children dressed in traditional costume: (left to right)
Walter Jr., Marie-José, Stance, Anton (on floor), Koert.

Koert, Marie-José, Anton, Stance, Walter Jr., circa 1928.

Left to right, Walter Jr. (Koert's older brother) & Koert, probably circa 1930.

Younger sister Charlotte with Koert in uniform (may have been in Dutch Army).

Studying.

Koert, probably mid-1930's.

Studying medicine at the University of Amsterdam.

Mr. Walter Baars (standing), Sitting around Koert (from left): Stance, Charlotte, Marie-José, Walter Jr.'s wife Miethes, Walter Jr.

Koert at a dinner party in Rotterdam (others pictured unknown),
November 27, 1941.

In his early twenties.

Koert and his sister Marie-José, with little
Volendam girl (1940's). Volendam is a small
town in Holland in which the residents, mostly
for the sake of the tourists, dress in traditional
period costume.

Koert and Mary Jean on their honeymoon (April 1948).

Koert and Mary Jean at their wedding reception: Oak Park, Illinois, April 3, 1948. His mother's photograph is in left foreground. His family could not make it from the Netherlands.

Family portrait circa 1962: Sue, Mary Jean, Ellie, Koert, Michael.

"The 3 American Baarses" — California, April 1952: Koert & Mary Jean with son Michael (Koert is Captain in U.S. Army).

Reliving life on the Dutch canals? (pulling son Michael and friend, winter, 1956-57, Rochester, Minnesota).

Koert in his office, circa 1978-79.

Koert and Mary Jean, Christmas, 1980.

"Well, it happened just by chance," he said. "One day I mixed some drugs together and injected them into a patient suffering from some illness, not tuberculosis. Imagine my horror when the man fell into a state of shock! Fortunately, he recovered in about fifteen minutes. Then I diluted the mixture and for no special reason injected it again into a patient with lung tuberculosis. Some time later I thought I noticed some improvement in his condition. Receiving the injection a few times more the man finally completely recovered!" He related this calmly, enjoying my amazement.

"Leo," I exclaimed, "Do you realize what it means if this is true?" Then the words seemed to pour out of me in excitement. "If it is really true, if you have found a way to completely cure this terrible disease, I know at last one reason God permitted these fiendish camps to exist. The miseries and death of the millions of our fellow prisoners would all have some meaning through such a wonderful discovery! Health and happiness would be brought back to many more millions of people all over the world, to people who otherwise would have to resign themselves and eventually succumb to the devastation of their disease." I stopped, out of breath after this outburst.

Leo had smiled at the mention of God's name but he had not interrupted me. Then he went on to tell me of the many patients, his own countrymen, whom he had already cured. There was no doubt in his mind of the efficiency of his newly discovered drug. But it seemed too freakish to be true, and I was far from convinced of his claim even after seeing some of the men supposedly cured by Leo.

Eagerly I begged him to treat one of my own countrymen who was in our ward in the final stage of tuberculosis. To see him cured would really do away with my skepticism. But Leo refused. He wanted to treat only his Polish patients. He felt he could trust no stranger to refrain from talking about his special treatments and eventual cure. Besides, there had been too many successful results already from his experiments. Some of his personal friends who had been admitted to ward nine, the "death ward," had been cured, and the Kapo of the hospital was getting suspicious. Leo's greatest fear was that the S.S. might hear of it, and he could be certain they would leave no means untouched to force the secret from him. The information, once obtained, would ensure his immediate death. Then a miraculous drug would be proclaimed to the world as a discovery of Germany's great men of science!

But one afternoon Leo came in and called me aside. "Come and examine a new patient of mine before I treat him with my drug. This is going to be my last cure," he said. "So now you have your opportunity and you will see. I shall prove to you my drug works."

As I examined the Polish patient, it was easy to see that the man was in an advanced state of tuberculosis of the lung. My physical examination revealed the presence of a large cavity in one of his lungs. His sputum had been found positive for the presence of the tubercle bacilli, but even though I agreed with this report, I did not have much confidence in the Czech who handled the laboratory work in the hospital. He was fully capable of doing this job, but permitted politics and intrigues to penetrate into the laboratory. Several times I had Czech patients whom I highly suspected of having open lung tuberculosis, but their reports always came back negative. Then one day I sent the same samples to the laboratory, only this time labelled with names not of Czech origin. As I suspected, they returned marked "positive." Obviously the technician wanted to protect his countrymen by keeping them from the dreaded death ward. A deed noble in itself, but extremely dangerous to the other patients, who would be easily infected in the crowded, unhygienic quarters of the camp.

But the results were worse when the Czech reversed his procedure and sent back sputum reports of non-Czech names marked "positive," although there would be no evidence of open tuberculosis in my examinations. Once a positive report was given, there was nothing that could be done to keep the patient from ward nine.

So in this important case, to be absolutely sure the Pole had lung tuberculosis, I took him to the X-ray department in the main hospital. There I saw without a doubt two large cavities and several small ones in his lungs. Then I asked Leo if I could watch him give the injection. I wanted to see for myself what reaction it would cause, if any. But he refused. Even in my disappointment I could not blame him much. Everyone distrusted everyone else, and with such a tremendously important secret to guard, it would be necessary to take every precaution. How could Leo know that I would not kill him to become the owner of the drug, or that I would not tell the S.S. in case I would happen to be executed and wanted to drag Leo with me in my misfortune? No, I did not blame Leo for being careful. I was surprised that he had let me in on his discovery at all.

After a few weeks Leo asked me to examine the Pole again. During the preceding days I had already noticed a marked improvement in the general appearance of the patient, especially his gain in weight, something which was extremely rare in the hospital even among the non-tubercular patients. Trying not to act too inquisitive, I had kept from examining the sick man. Now I eagerly began testing the patient. Over and over again I repeated my examination. Try as I might, I could not find anything to indicate any cavity in his lungs! Auscultation revealed that there were still some pathological processes going on in the lungs, but that was all that was evident.

Once more Leo and I took him to the X-ray room. There I saw what I had hardly dared to believe. The cavities were gone! They were actually healed with only a few scars covering their former openings. The roentgenologist, a Frenchman, and a very able specialist, was amazed too. But Leo and I pretended to be unconcerned, and covered up by saying that the previous examination must have been a mistake.

A week later the Polish patient was transferred to a ward in the main hospital and due to a newly developing animosity between the Frenchman in charge and me, I was not able to follow the case further. Later I heard that the patient had been discharged from the hospital altogether! Now I was really convinced of the miraculous action of Leo's drug, because the normal contributory factors for the healing of a tuberculous lung process were simply non-existent in Buchenwald. Patients with this disease need bed rest, sunlight, good nursing care and a well-balanced diet. Therefore this patient could not have been cured by the ordinary, inadequate means we had there.

Realizing that this tremendous discovery must get out of the camp at any cost, I proposed to Leo that he share his knowledge with two others whom he could trust. Thus in the event of his death, a possibility always to be considered, at least one or both of the others could reveal his secret to the world. Leo agreed with me and decided to tell the composition of the drug to Sulikov, as he was very friendly with this Russian doctor because of their mutual political ideals. Naturally, I considered Sulikov a very unfortunate choice.

Leo would also share the secret with me, for he knew I was only interested in its value to the medical world and mankind, and not in the possible material benefit that would befall the discoverer of this priceless drug. But he had no intention of revealing it until the last moment, at the time of a mass murder of the prisoners or a general evacuation. I had to accept his decision. Less than a year later, when we were liberated by the American forces, Leo and the Russian doctor Sulikov disappeared in the confusion, leaving me without the formula and without a hint of their whereabouts.[1]

---

[1] Since my arrival in America I have been in frequent correspondence with Leo. He has taken up the study of medicine and works in a hospital in Poland. One of his chiefs there, a Polish doctor, fled the country after having learned part of the formula, probably assuming that he could easily discover the rest. Leo, being in need of money and food, offered to sell me the formula for a very reasonable price. I contacted one of the largest American pharmaceutical houses, but its representatives refused to gamble a few hundred dollars on what they probably considered a myth. As I could not raise the money myself, Leo decided to take a patent on his discovery and according to the latest news the formula is now being fully tested in one of the Polish research laboratories. Let us hope that the world will soon hear of this wonderful drug. Polish newspapers have carried the news about this drug, but so far it has not been publicized outside of the Iron Curtain. [The events described in this note seem to have taken place in the late 1940's. Nothing further seems to have been heard about this drug.]

≥ *19* ≤

Johnny was a tall, warm-hearted Negro, who showed his contempt for the bad elements in the camp so openly that this eventually sent him to "Dora," the deadliest of Buchenwald's commandos. Johnny worked in the hospital as a skin specialist, although he confessed to me that he had never studied medicine and that he had been a cabaret artist in the nightclubs of Paris. Johnny had a wonderful gift for story-telling, and many of our dark days were brightened by his flights of fancy into the world we once knew.

When we had some R.A.F. prisoners in the ward, Johnny told about his imaginary experiences as a pilot of an American bomber. He told a wild and wonderful story, and we were all right there with him doing our part to carry out a successful raid. The R.A.F. fellows had a lot of fun listening to him and laughing at the numerous tactical mistakes that he made in the telling. He would wave his long arms and bob his small head as the story got more exciting.

It was good to be near him, for his spontaneous gaiety was a welcome relief from the dark despondency that filled our lives. He was sympathetic to his fellow prisoners, and always gave their morale a lift with his friendly cheerfulness. No one doubted the sincerity of his attitude, for if he disliked a person or their actions, he let it be known. If you were his friend, you did not have to look for the hidden reason. Here in the camp one was friendly in order to gain something — and we all kept the friendly ones at a distance until we had discovered their motives. But not Johnny. We knew his friendship was genuine.

Johnny's frankness in naming his enemies and condemning their unjust actions was dangerous for him. In Buchenwald, a prisoner who cared for his life silently watched every other inmate to try to learn the situation before uttering a word. So it was heartbreaking to watch Johnny throw himself on the mercy of his unmerciful enemies, for the very ones he antagonized were in a position of authority to eliminate him. But that did not stop him. Soon he was not only endangering his own life, but that of his friends. I tried desperately to show him how he was hurting himself, but my pleading was in vain. Several times the Kapo warned me to keep away from my friend — or else.

Ever since I had met Johnny, I had been saving bread for him. He was always ravenous — as we all were, but his big body seemed to need more food than that of others. After I had received three or four threatening messages to avoid him, I had to smuggle the bread to him after dark.

Once when he became sick and had to stay in bed, I brought him a jar of molasses syrup, which he always liked. His appreciation was worth any risk I had taken.

"Koert," he said, "I've been lying here thinking of that stuff."

Just then the prisoner-chief of the canteen came running over to us.

"What's the idea of stealing the syrup from your own patients to give to this one?" he shouted at me.

I felt no guilt whatsoever for having taken the syrup, for none of my patients wanted it because of the terrific diarrhea it caused. It didn't bother Johnny at all.

"My patients don't want it," I said to the angry chief.

"It's not for him then. I'll tell you something: if you are seen with this man again, you'll be in big trouble!" I knew this was no idle threat: as a Communist he had considerable power. The next morning I heard that Johnny was to be sent to "Dora," and that same afternoon I was ordered to appear before S.S. Hauptsturmfuehrer Dr. Rogge. Somebody, I readily could guess who, had presented me for this same dreaded transport. My enemies wanted me out of the way — not because I was dangerous to them; for that I was too unimportant — but I had a greatly desired job, which the Communist prisoners wanted for one of their own.

So I stood before Dr. Rogge, fearful of what this sudden questioning might bring. Just before I had learned that a doctor was needed on this transport but no nurses. So when the doctor asked me if I was a qualified physician, I decided to play for high stakes. I denied it boldly.

The S.S. officer looked at the Kapo, who was staring at me in astonishment and said, "But his record shows he is a physician."

I blurted, hoarse with tension, "They must have misunderstood me at the first questioning; I am just a medical student."

Dr. Rogge shrugged his shoulders, "Well, then I cannot use you. I need a doctor. You may go."

I waited while the Kapo changed my record where it said "physician" to say "medical student." Then I left the office. I felt that I had outwitted my enemies for the time being, but I was still apprehensive about their next move — and mine. I knew that they would eliminate me as soon as they found a way.

It was well known in the camp that the Communist prisoners, who under the S.S. were in charge of the camp, made up 99% of the list of names of those to go on the transports. A transport was not always a bad thing, but one never knew what hell it might bring. I had a good place in the hospital, and I knew how to get along there.

The thought of a transport and of the bullying I had just taken sent me that very day to one of the prominent Communists in the camp. He was the Kapo of the pathology department and before the war an engineer in Austria. I had met him several times before and knew him to be an honest man, who respected and considered even my opinions. I told him frankly about the intrigues the Communist prisoners plotted against me.

He listened attentively and promised to talk with the Kapo of the hospital who, as the official Communist representative to the German Reichstag in pre-Hitler days, was a good friend of his. That night he assured me that unless the S.S. interfered, my name would be kept off the transport lists. I knew then that I was relatively safe from the machinations of his own party-comrades.

It was a peculiar situation that I, a Catholic, had to be protected from the Communist prisoners by their own powerful leaders. It also shows that a Communist as an individual does not necessarily have to be an evil person, provided that he has an open and respectful ear for the ideologies of others, and that he does not follow the orders and commands from the Kremlin blindly. But then, such a person would not be a good Communist in the sense the Kremlin wants him to be.

Well, the two Kapos who protected me from Communist intrigues were not good Communists. God bless them for that!

⋙ 20 ⋘

A French physician took the place of Alex, the Russian "doctor," who had been eliminated from the quarantine hospital. At first I was happy about the new man because the sick needed a qualified doctor. Then, too, I would be able to learn something from him and to discuss the many interesting medical cases scientifically. I knew this doctor only from seeing him at the weekly rollcalls for hospital personnel. At these calls, he was an interpreter for the Russians. His father was French and his mother Russian, so he spoke the Russian language fluently.

I welcomed him warmly into our ward, thinking of the improvements that would come with him. I told him at once that I was a medical student and had no doctor's degree, the University having been closed just before I was to take the final examinations. The S.S. knew now that the original statement on my record that I was a qualified physician had been wrong, so I was taking no chance by telling him my true rating. It might help to have him know that I was a willing student eager to work and learn under him. I was genuinely enthusiastic about furthering my medical knowledge with his help.

But from the beginning he seemed to have a feeling of animosity toward me. He was careful not to show it openly, which technique was part of the usual tactics of all prisoners — not to fight in the open. I never could find out the reason for his hostility toward me. I thought perhaps it might be that he resented my telling him about certain medical procedures in Holland. He usually would ignore this information I gave him and never would discuss it with me as I had hoped he would. The opportunity for stimulating conversation was rare here, and I had thought that we would at least enjoy that pleasure. However, he was always reticent with me, and his orders were concise and conclusive. I do not know whether his personal or his national pride was hurt by my suggestions.

My greatest disappointment in this man was his extreme partiality toward the French patients. He would always look to them first, leaving the others, including some who needed prompt attention, to wait — sometimes until the next day. His favoritism was understandable, but certainly not just. A doctor should never show preference among race, religion, or nationality in his regard for a patient; a patient is a person in need of medical help, be he Rumanian, Greek Orthodox, or an Afro-American Baptist. I had always tried to be strictly impartial, so his actions went against the grain with me. One day I made the mistake of telling the doctor that I thought his conduct was unethical. He was outraged. A Dutch student preaching ethics to a French doctor: it was unthinkable!

From then on, he spoke as little as possible to me. The only time he seemed to notice me was when he gave me orders. Leo, who was completely on my side, did not get the same treatment as I did. Although the doctor considered him a medical illiterate and treated him accordingly much to Leo's annoyance, he did not antagonize him. The doctor was aware of the influence Leo had in the politics in the camp.

After this complete breakdown in our relationship, the doctor had a French medical student, who was a nurse in charge of another ward, come to our ward for daily conferences with him and Richet, who had once been a professor of physiology at the Sorbonne in Paris and now was the doctor for the other barrack of the quarantine hospital. They examined all of the interesting cases, even the patients who were at the point of death — the ones Leo and I tried to keep undisturbed. It was ideal bedside teaching for the student. Leo and I began to take care of the sick who were overlooked by the doctor. It was hard to take care of the many men, so sometimes we forgot to do what the doctor ordered. My negligence about the doctor's orders gave him an excuse to get me replaced by his French student.

It was July 20th, one of Buchenwald's rare sunny days. Having used the afternoon rest period to take a sun bath, I returned to the ward to dress. The doctor was sitting at the table by the door with his head in his hands. When he saw me, he jumped up and shouted:

"You are a lazy no-good. You would let my patients die in front of your nose!" He was frantic. Furious at his words, I began to shout back at him, but he slapped me heavily on the cheek. As I was trying to get into my pants at the time, I nearly fell over, but quickly he hit me on the other cheek and broke my fall. The blood rushed to my head, and I stumbled around to regain my balance. My situation was ridiculous as I finally fumbled into my pants. My indignation was tremendous, and I was eager to get my hands on him. There was nothing I wanted to do more at that moment than to give that man what he had coming. Fortunately, he left the room before I could recover enough to return his blows. As I calmed down, I noticed Leo standing near.

"I saw everything, Koert. If he had done that to me, I would have stabbed him to death," Leo said.

Then the doctor returned. My temper had cooled some, and I was relieved that I hadn't had the chance to strike back at him. There were better ways of settling an argument, and besides, I remembered now that the chief Kapo of the hospital, the former Communist representative to the Reichstag, was greatly opposed to fighting and beating. Some hospital workers who had been caught fighting had been sent to the quarry as punishment. Insults were more bearable than that.

So when the doctor came back and self-righteously announced that he had told Hermann, the Kapo, the whole story (his side of it, of course), I ran out to find Hermann before any action could be taken. He was about to go to the chief Kapo of the hospital to report the situation. I begged him to listen to my explanation, but it was obvious that Hermann believed the Frenchman's accusations against me, and he set out for the main hospital.

I rushed back to my ward and asked Leo to go quickly to

Hermann and explain the circumstances. He left at once, and I watched him overtake Hermann at the entrance of the hospital.

Waiting nervously for Leo's return, I was hardly able to go on with my work intelligently. I could not keep from thinking of the danger my life would be in if the chief Kapo did not believe my story. I would surely be sent to the quarry and lose my good commando here in the hospital. In my weakened physical condition at this time I would have a hard time getting through the bitter winter months in that hell. I was exhausted with worry by the time Leo returned. But I could tell at first glance at him that everything was all right — he was smiling. I sighed deeply to myself while I listened to the details of the interview with Hermann and the chief Kapo.

The outcome was that I was to exchange wards with the French student, and Leo was to keep an eye on both the doctor and his protege. The doctor openly showed his disappointment that I had not been sent to the quarry. He was content, though, to have his French student with him.

Although I was safe from the quarry, I was angry that my name had been brought into serious disrepute, and I decided to try to get back my good professional standing. This could be done only by having the doctor, for whom I had lost all respect, sent on a transport. But fortunately I did nothing myself to accomplish this, for as much as I had against him, I did not want to be the cause of his death. I would have had that on my conscience forever. It happened that it took only weeks before Leo's reports of the doctor's unscrupulous conduct sent him on a transport to the Ruhr area. And so I was rehabilitated. The French patients in my old ward who had been against me a short time before were so very friendly now!

In the meantime, I had been put in a 24-bed ward for contagious diseases in the other quarantine hospital barrack. Here stooped, white-haired, sixty-eight year old Professor Charles Richet of the Sorbonne was the attending doctor. His first words to me were not flattering.

"It is about time you started to work hard and not be so lazy."

"Professor," I said, "you are prejudiced, I am afraid. I think you have been listening to my enemies."

He let me prove that I was a good worker, and eventually I took over the majority of his work when he became too weak. I was very fond of Richet, and so were his patients, for he treated them with utmost tenderness. He went out of his way to bring sugar to the weakest, and he would have an encouraging greeting for the depressed. But most important of all, there was no national nor racial discrimination in his attitude toward the sick men who depended on him.

We had many interesting discussions, for he was a stimulating conversationalist. It was rare to find anyone here who wanted to talk about anything but his immediate surrounding and food. It was especially good to know someone who wanted to talk about medicine. Of course, we compared notes on the diagnosis, and once in a while we did not agree. Some of these disagreements turned into friendly but real arguments, and these debates were delightful to me, although often I would be too blunt and positive in my statements and Richet would get angry and call me "monsieur." But it was not in his nature to stay angry long, and soon he would return to calling me the usual "mon cher."

When in a confidential mood, he would tell me how annoyed he was that he, a professor of fame at the Sorbonne, had to take orders from people who had never had any medical education. I myself often was disgusted about this, but I did not forget that it had been the simple and poorly educated German prisoners in the first years of the camp who had built the hospital with their own hands under great trouble and with serious opposition from the S.S. It had been these same prisoners who had expanded it to the 2500-bed hospital of the present time. The hospital now had two well-equipped operating rooms, a laboratory, an X-ray and a physical therapy department, all partly equipped with instruments stolen from Buchenwald's S.S. hospital.

As in the first years of Buchenwald's existence, professional men were not allowed into the hospital; these untrained prisoners had even operated themselves. They could not be reproached that many of their patients died under the knife. Some of them had acquired great dexterity. One prisoner, a bicycle repairer, had become a specialist in operating on and treating phlegmons — widespread abscesses of the soft tissues of the body or extremities — and a disease which killed many thousand emaciated prisoners.

Another prisoner, a baker by trade, could hardly be bettered by a doctor in his performance of a pneumothorax — artificial collapse of a lung in patients with tuberculosis. Another, a German cook, had learned and mastered the simpler methods of laboratory technique. All of them had not unwillingly given a place to the professional men when finally the S.S. allowed them to work in the hospital.

What could be done by these medically untrained men was most evident in the morgue of the camp. Here worked side by side a German criminal, convicted of several murders, and a Czech Catholic priest, both performing autopsies with extreme dexterity while a French pathologist took care of the official autopsy reports. The Czech priest, a highly esteemed man, had received his education in this branch of medicine in the concentration camp of Auschwitz in Poland where the gas chambers had provided him with more material than any medical school in the world ever could have offered to its students!

So I kept quiet when Richet spoke of these uneducated men who ordered him about. The good French doctor's daily visits to my ward were always amusing, as he insisted on everyone observing the proprieties due his title and age. If a patient kept on with his talking, eating or sleeping during Richet's visits, he would deliver a penitential sermon in French or broken German, whether the patient understood or not. When he had finished scolding, he would turn to me and say with a voice full of indignation, "That is unbecoming, isn't it so, Koert?"

But he was soon pleasant again and sympathetically made

his rounds, hobbling along on legs stiff from rheumatism. It took longer and longer for him to make his visits as his affliction became more severe. Eventually he could no longer complete a routine visit, but he would always come and put his head inside the door and wave to the patients, and say to me, "Everybody is all right? Excellent! Good-bye."

Before I had time to answer him, he would shuffle off. But we were left with the spirit of comfort that came from his good heart. I worked under this old gentleman for only a few months, but in that time I saw how his encouragement buoyed up the morale of the suffering patient.

After these months the professor was assigned to my old ward with Leo. The new doctor of my ward became Sulikov, who committed the most cold-blooded murders of his fellow prisoners that I had ever seen or heard of.

My good days with Richet were over; I should need their remembrances to get me sanely through the next months, under the murdering Russian Sulikov.

≥ 21 ≤

Forgetting the danger, I stood at the door of the barrack to look up at the stately moving squadron high in the air. Smaller planes flew close to the earth at terrifying speed.

At this moment I wished desperately to be up there in the sky helping my friends instead of merely waiting for the German defeat. My heart leaped at the magnificent sight of powerful planes carrying free men high over this dark pit of misery. How close they were, and yet how immeasurably far away! I wondered how soon it would be that these free men reached our gates by land.

It was August 24th, 1944. The air-raid sirens had howled their warning through the camp just a few minutes before. The S.S. had scampered to their hideouts, the first-aid troop of German prisoners had gone to their posts, and the prisoners who worked inside the camp had run into their barracks as ordered.

Eight thousand prisoners who worked in the "Gustloff" factories, where guns, ammunition, and airplane accessories were being made, had no place to go but to the open fields surrounding the factories. Four thousand prisoners, who worked on the parts of the notorious V-1 and V-2 bombs, were allowed to leave the six large halls of the "Mibeu" factories.

This interruption would not delay the German war production much, because sabotage by the prisoners had fixed it so that during the last year eighty percent of the guns had been declared unfit by S.S. engineers, not one cable used in the V-1 and V-2 bombs had been approved, and it took twenty times longer than necessary to make a munition wagon.

And so the men of Buchenwald waited for the bombs to fall. The prisoners and their keepers were equal now under the blue sky. As the last screams of the sirens bounced in our ears, hell came down from heaven. Explosions were all about us. The barracks trembled. The patients in the ward were lying under their beds. The lamps fell from the ceiling, the doors sprang open, and the glass from the windows rained in splinters on everything. The iron containers of the incendiary bombs bounced on the barrack roof and clattered on the ground. Explosions bellowed near us, and then the fires rose high in the wind. I continued to watch as the dark smoke clouded the clear sky.

Our friends had not forgotten us — they knew there was a Buchenwald, although to us inside it had seemed that no one knew, that the world came no farther than the barbed wire. But today it was clear that they were well acquainted with the existence of the camp. They knew Buchenwald foot by foot. For when the raid was over, the factories, garages, and houses of the S.S. officers had been destroyed, and not one prisoners' barracks had been hit, in spite of the fact that some of the factory buildings were in close proximity to the camp's barbed wire fences.

As soon as the planes had gone, everyone ran from cover to help with the casualties. A few prisoner barracks had caught fire as the strong wind had blown the flames into the camp. I hurried outside to help where the factories blazed. When I got to the iron entrance gates, they were open and the guards who stood there day and night had this time left their post. I looked up and saw that the towers around the camp were empty, and no German trained his machine gun down on us. It was natural to think of escaping, but I knew that once free of the camp there would be no place to go. We were in the heart of Nazi Germany, far away from the Swiss border. There would be no help coming from the hostile Germans in the villages. Besides, the picture of the prisoners who some time ago had made an unsuccessful escape was still too vivid in my mind. They had been choked to death on the gallows in the middle of the square which served as the site for the morning and evening roll-calls.

Another nurse and I picked up a stretcher and went out through the gates. Even the S.S. administration barrack just opposite the entrance of the gates had been hit and was in flames. S.S. and prisoners were already salvaging the furniture. The S.S. Commander of the camp stomped back and forth in front of the barrack, gesticulating wildly to his staff officers. He did not see us as we walked by without giving the obligatory salute of removing our cap or turning our head in military fashion. The S.S. now had more vital worries than unsaluting prisoners.

An S.S. man ran up to us and told us to get to the forest for the wounded and dead. We looked around to find the way. This was the first time we had been outside of the gate since our arrival, and we did not know the layout. We could have used one of our flying friends' maps! The road was blocked, and we saw no way of getting to the forest except by climbing in and out of the windows of the burning S.S. barrack.

Flames and smoke covered everything. We moved in the direction of the long line of wounded prisoners who were headed for the camp. The roads were covered with stones and rubbish from the ruins of the huge factories which still burned furiously. The wounded prisoners returning for help became more numerous, and they directed us to the place where the more seriously hurt were lying.

On our way we passed an S.S. officer sitting on a pile of stones and crying for help. My companion started to go to him, but I pulled him along with me.

"First our fellow prisoners and then the S.S.," I said. I could not forget hearing a friend quoting the German Red Cross women who, after the bombardment of Weimar, where many of Buchenwald's prisoners had been killed and wounded, had said, "Oh, they are only prisoners! They don't need help." Thus our friends were left under the rubble dying until prisoner hospital workers could get to them. This time it would be our own comrades first.

Hurrying from one wounded man to another, we gave first-aid to those who still showed signs of life, however seriously they had been wounded by shrapnel. The ground was like a battlefield, covered with wide shell holes, snapped-off trees, and thousands of holes made by incendiary bombs. Heads, bodies, arms and legs were strewn about. This leg belonged to an S.S. man, for there was a boot on the foot. This head belonged to a prisoner, for it was shaved bald. And here was a prisoner in a zebra striped uniform lying in brotherly fashion next to the S.S. man on whose shining belt buckle were the words, "Gott mit uns."

Then I found one of my Dutch friends dead with a split skull. A few minutes later, I saw my good friend Dolf sitting pale and quiet near a mound of dirt. Fortunately he was not hurt. Later he told me that many of the prisoners had been shot by the S.S. at the beginning of the raid. Trying to get to safety from the falling bombs, they had fled in panic in all directions, thereby passing unintentionally and without thought of escape the chain of S.S. guards who always formed a huge circle around the camp and the neighboring grounds. It had been mainly the Ukrainian S.S. who had done this cowardly shooting. It was so cruel that even a few of the German S.S. men had shot the Ukrainian S.S. men on the spot!

After a few hours of work, giving first-aid and caring for the badly wounded, I returned to my ward and either discharged or transferred all my patients. That evening there were twenty-four victims of the bombing in my ward. Those who had lost arms or legs had to be taken care of immediately, and they took our full attention during the long night.

Four hundred prisoners had died as a result of the raid. Two hundred Nazi men and a hundred and fifty Nazi women, among whom were the Commander's wife and daughter, were killed. But most important of all, the camp's war production had been completely paralyzed. The raid had been a masterful feat. It had been one of those bombardments of which the German radio would say again:

"An unsuccessful raid made by our enemies. Only some cows killed and various churches destroyed."

All thirteen halls of the "Gustloff" factories, all six halls of the "Mibeu" factories, the huge garages where daily hundreds of cars and trucks were repaired, and many houses of the S.S. officers had been destroyed. And not one explosive or incendiary bomb had fallen in the camp itself. How well the fliers knew their work. How accurate were their maps, how exactly fell the bombs on their targets. The men of peace had brought the war back to its home, from where Goering had bawled, "No English plane will ever come over German territory!"

⇒ 22 ⇐

Dark-haired Sulikov, a Georgian Russian, was the doctor in charge of my ward in the quarantine hospital in the early months of 1945. It was the time when the Germans were emptying the concentration camps in the paths of the Allies. Of the thousands of prisoners that were herded into Buchenwald, hundreds needed hospitalization. Our wards were even more crowded than they had been before. Medicine was scarce, and the beds held twice their intended load. We could have used a qualified and tireless physician in our ward. Sulikov was not that. I soon saw that his title of doctor did not at all correspond to his abilities. I imagine that he was a first or second year medical student who, like so many, was after a job with more food and so a better chance to survive. To "Dr." Sulikov, it meant also the opportunity to practice murder — for murder was his method of liquidating his enemies: those who were opposed to Communism.

I did not realize this Russian's criminal tendencies until later when the frequency with which Roland, my French "kalfactor," was being ordered to carry corpses to the dead-house, aroused my suspicions. True, death here was continual, but these new deaths were far above the expected number, and they all occurred in the showers of the hospital. It was routine to give all the new arrivals a shower before admitting them to the wards, and occasionally this would prove too much for some old prisoner worn out by illness and starvation.

The next time a group of patients was brought to the ward to be admitted, I waited around until they were put in the showers. I wanted to discover what was going on before I asked any questions and put myself on the spot. As the prisoners filed into the room, I looked over the papers on the table. Just then

Sulikov walked into the hall and looked at me inquisitively as I pretended to be reading a record card. I thought he was going to speak to me, but just then I heard the water turn on in the room, and Sulikov went on in. I glanced up quickly and thought I saw a syringe in his hands. When I returned to my own ward, Roland was called away to carry nine bodies from the showers. My suspicion was complete. I could not get my mind off of the horrible idea that this Russian who pretended to be a doctor was killing at will. I tried to imagine that these deaths were caused by something else. When the next group of sick arrived to be admitted, I had another chance to find out more. This time I kept out of sight as I watched the prisoners put through the routine of admittance. After they had gone into the bathroom, Sulikov went in as before. I knew that I had seen a syringe in his hand, but there was still one more bit of information I must find — a most important bit: what was in that syringe. I went back to my ward, and after Roland had been ordered to his gruesome duty of carrying the freshly dead and had returned, I went back to the admittance hall. As no one was around, I went on into the recently used showers. I looked hurriedly around and found the syringe lying on the table.

Near it was an ampule containing a solution of arsenic! I could hardly contain my wrath. It took all of my self-restraint to hide my indignation, and yet I could do nothing nor tell anyone, though I burned inside at the miserable thought of the inhuman acts that went on every day so close to me. If Sulikov and his accomplices had any idea that I knew of their murders, I would have been as easily disposed of as any of their victims. So I could tell no one of what I knew, and there was no way to stop these pernicious men. Violence ruled here. It was the method of these Communists who had maneuvered for power over the prisoners of the camp to liquidate their opposition brutally but effectively.

The next day I watched the hideous performance in the bathroom through a window. Two seconds after the solution of arsenic had been injected into the poor victim who was lying on

the floor, a terrific convulsion of the whole body had made an end
to his life.

The days went on slowly as always. I could not keep my
mind off the nightmarish scene of murder. I hated myself for not
being able to do something to stop the crimes. My only consolation was that many of the prisoners who were given the Sulikov
treatment were already doomed before they entered the hospital,
as their physical condition was so poor that the inadequate
medicine we had would have helped them little. And yet, even so,
has one man the right to take the life of another? Life — it was our
only possession here in Buchenwald. If Sulikov's killing was
done out of mercy, it was still a serious sin to me. But I knew better
than to consider this angle, even to rationalize myself into a more
peaceable state of mind.

Within a day or two of my hideous discovery, I was called
in to see Hermann, the Kapo. He was a Communist who had
spent twelve years in prisons and concentration camps. He had
had much experience in that time in learning how to survive and
how to grow in power in this kind of society.

I, too, had become hardened by the endless suffering around
me, but not hard and bitter enough to experience no repugnance
at having to put up with such a degenerate individual as this
Russian. This was more than I could take, although I was condi-
tioned to atrocity by now. It seemed almost impossible to associate sanely with this Communist madman.

Hermann wanted my advice about a 55-year-old Russian
patient who was in my ward with pellagra, one of the vitamin
deficiency diseases. This patient suffered a serious intestinal
disturbance, characteristic of this disease, and he was too weak to
leave his bed. His condition made the whole ward disagreeable
to the other patients. Hermann asked me how long I thought this
patient could be expected to live.

"I don't think more than a week," I replied.

"Do you think that there is any chance that he might
recover?" he asked again.

"Humanly speaking, no. It would be impossible," I answered. "It would be a miracle if he lives." I tried to figure out what was behind all this sudden interest in the case. His next question made his purpose only too clear.

"Will you give him an injection?"

"No, Hermann," I said, "That I will not do!"

He looked very surprised and wanted to know if I liked the spoiled atmosphere caused by the patient's intestinal disturbance.

"No, on the contrary; especially for the other patients. It is more unpleasant for them than for me, as I don't need to be in the ward every moment of the day."

"Well, why don't you give him a few tablets that will make an end to this situation? You yourself just stated that it is impossible for him to recover," he said calmly.

There I was being asked to become a member of their murder crew! Or did they think euthanasia is not murder? It was not difficult to make a decision even though I realized that refusing to cooperate with this demand could put me in grave danger. Still, I preferred this than to go through the rest of my life with a murder on my conscience.

"Hermann," I said, "I know that you are a Communist and that you do not believe in the existence of a God, but you know that I am a Catholic and as such I do believe in a God. My religion does not allow me to shorten a man's life that was given him by God, even though this may be intended to help him out of unbearable sufferings. Besides, I hope to be a doctor one day if we shall get out of this camp, and as such I intend to cure men, not kill them. If you or others want to do what you just now proposed, I cannot prevent you from doing so as you are the most powerful here, but I refuse to give you my assistance."

He shrugged his shoulders and I was allowed to go. For a long time I lived in constant fear that I would have to suffer the consequences of my refusal, but nothing happened. Never again was I asked to participate in their "murder incorporated"!

The Russian died the next day. I found one tablet in his bed that I had not given to him.

Not only old and incurable prisoners were killed by our Communist fellow prisoners. One evening in February 1945, during the general roll-call from which only the hospital personnel were exempted, I went to the erysipelas ward where two Czech nurses were in command. With the oldest of them I played chess, the only pastime we could indulge in during our free moments. During one game that night, one of the patients joined occasionally in the conversation of the onlookers, who were mostly Czech. I also heard him speak in French with some of the other patients. One of the onlookers asked me in German to speak some English with that patient as he had boasted to be able to speak seven languages, and he would like to know if this were true. Before I could reply, the patient who had heard this question addressed me in fluent English, though with a slight accent. I was surprised and told him that I would like to see him when the game was finished.

Later he told me that he was Russian, born in Georgia, and had traveled widely throughout the world. For many years he had lived in America, where he had been employed with Metro-Goldwyn-Mayer as a stage manager. Shortly before the war, he had gone to France in connection with the production of a new film, by the name of "Treasure," if I remember well. At some time during the war, he had been arrested by the Germans and had been sent to the concentration camp of Sachsenhausen, near Berlin. Only a few days before, this camp had been evacuated for fear of the quickly approaching Russian army, and most of the prisoners had been transferred to Buchenwald.

As all the patients in this ward suffered from erysipelas, and I at first glance could detect no trace of this illness in him, I asked what was the matter with him.

"Oh nothing at all," he replied. "I am in perfect health, but somebody I met here helped me escape the horrible conditions of the quarantine camp."

I congratulated him on the fact that he had such good friends and asked him whom his friend might be.

"Sulikov, one of my own countrymen," he replied. "He is also from Georgia and has promised me the job of hospital nurse as soon as my official time in the quarantine camp will have elapsed."

Another Communist, I thought, and the pleasure I had experienced speaking English with this well-educated and interesting person disappeared as snow in the sun. But I had been prejudiced, for when I inquired why and when he had left Russia, he answered, "I was a White Russian and I had to get out of Russia at the beginning of the Bolshevik Revolution." I was highly amazed at this as I could not understand this friendship between him and Sulikov, the murdering Communist. I did not dare ask more questions, but intended to keep my eyes and ears open to learn more about this perplexing situation. I wished him goodnight and promised to return to see him the next day. I considered it a welcome opportunity to speak English again, and more so a chance to be able to learn about the country I had always wanted to go to, America.

As I had not understood Victor's last name well, I went through the pile of patient's records to see if I could find one that might be his. I discovered the card lying all by itself on another table. When one of the Czech nurses found me with the card in my hands, I asked him in a casual way what the Russian was in for.

"Oh, that man, he is very ill," the Czech said.

"But why is his hospital record lying all by itself?" I could not refrain from asking, though I should have had enough experience to know that nosiness might be very unhealthy. A peculiar smile played around the lips of the Czech when he replied that the man was to be transferred to the main hospital the next morning for a severe operation. As I knew this man to be an ardent Communist, and I did not want to have him know that I did not believe his yarn, I left him with an, "Oh, I see." Had I known that I would receive a front row seat to the performance of a hideous drama, I would not have slept so well that night.

The next morning, on returning from the emergency room where I had taken care of a few patients, I found Sulikov in my ward. He was stirring in a cup some of the milk diet that was given to the patients who could not stand the daily ration of soup and bread. Though I thought this rather strange, I had no suspicions whatsoever, until he left my ward with the cup and I heard him go to the erysipelas ward. Suddenly I recalled my meeting with Victor the night before, and I got an uneasy feeling. As I could not leave my ward at that time, I asked Roland to go and see what Sulikov was doing and at the same time have a look at the Russian about whose ability to speak so many languages I had told him yesterday. About ten minutes later Roland returned and reported that Sulikov had given the cup with the milk diet to Victor. Then when Sulikov had left, Roland had gone to the patient and had asked him in French how he liked the food. "It was very good," he had answered, "only somewhat bitter, but I am so hungry and such good food I have not tasted for a long time."

Bitter, I thought, that is strange; usually that diet is not very sweet, but I could never call it bitter. However, since the quality of this diet had deteriorated in the last few months, I seldom ate my share of it, as I was not a great eater and seldom very hungry, though there were many patients and friends of mine who had a much harder life than I had who always welcomed it greatly. So I took it for granted that the diet had become bitter and forgot all about it until ten minutes later when I heard some noise outside in the corridor. I opened the door to see what was going on. With a flash everything became clear. The whole deceit was a cunning plan to get Victor into the hospital and so in their power.

There Victor walked, no, staggered between the two Czech nurses, while his "friend" and countryman Sulikov followed. Mumbling like a drunkard and with his eyes protruding from their sockets, Victor still seemed to recognize me.

I cried out to him in English, "Put your finger in your throat, try to vomit, you have been poisoned!" Then the four of them went quickly into the washroom. The door was locked. The sounds of struggling were loud, and I heard Victor shouting in the Russian language. The only thing I could understand was, "No, I won't sit down." Then the door was opened and they came out. Victor's eyes were glassy, and he was more carried by the nurses than walking. He gave me a look I shall never forget as long as I live, and which I am unable to describe, so sad and understanding it was.

They went to the emergency room where Victor probably was given the final injection of arsenic. I turned around, almost with tears in my eyes, not because I felt pity—I had seen too many die — but because I felt so utterly powerless against those criminals in whose eyes no human life was sacred unless it, too, was blinded by their pernicious ideal, Communism. A few minutes later Roland was called to bring another corpse to the morgue.

The official death report read: Victor Karumidse, deceased the 15th of February 1945. Immediate cause of death: sepsis due to erysipelas.

❧ 23 ❧

During the winter of '44-45, many thousands of Hungarian Jews arrived in Buchenwald, all evacuees from the various concentration camps in the east of Germany and Poland. It could not be said that they were an asset to the camp, nor to their country, nor to the Jewish race, among whom there were certainly many excellent and prominent characters. However, my first acquaintance with one of these prisoners was not an unpleasant one.

Hardly twenty years of age, this young Hungarian was a genius at playing the violin. Every night he spent as a patient in our ward, he played for us on an old borrowed violin. With his beautiful music he made us forget for awhile the misery around us. We all decided to do our best to help him escape the usual fate of the newly arriving prisoners — to be sent to one of the worst commandos.

On a Sunday we invited the bandmaster of Buchenwald's prisoner band to get his opinion on the talents of this young Jew. After the boy had played for a few minutes, the bandmaster became so enthusiastic that we knew that our brilliant patient would be safe for the time being. And indeed, he was given a light job as assistant to the chief of one of the Jewish barracks, which enabled him to save his hands that in the quarry or elsewhere might have been ruined irreparably. As he was a Jew, he was not allowed to join Buchenwald's illustrious band, which was mainly used to accompany the prisoners to and from their daily work with military marches. But in the pathology barrack, there were musicians who under the protection of the Austrian Communist — the same who had helped me so well — performed Sunday afternoon concerts for a small audience. Our protege was allowed to join this group; as the spiritual leader was the first violinist of the Conservatoire in Paris, he could not help but benefit from this artist's influence.

But eaten bread is soon forgotten. Never were we shown a sign of gratitude, in spite of the many tears of sorrow the young Hungarian genius had shed when he was discharged from our ward, in spite of all his assurances that he would never forget what we had done for him. It would have been such a little thing for him to invite us once in a while to one of their concerts, which would have given us so much pleasure and a time of blissful oblivion — only the melodies of a Mozart, a Beethoven, a Wagner and others could make us temporarily forget the bitterness inflicted upon us by their descendants, who had not hesitated to build their bloody murder camp around the famous tree under whose leaves Goethe once used to find inspiration for his works.

But I do not want to blame our protege too much; ingratitude was too common a trait among the prisoners. The virtue of gratitude did not fit into the struggle for life. But ingratitude does not pay off in the long run: as we lost all contact with the violinist, we were unable to save him on the day, shortly before our liberation, that all Jewish prisoners found a miserable death during their evacuation from our camp. His name will never be on the programs of the world's most famous concert halls; he must have found as gruesome a death as his parents, brothers and sisters found in the gas chambers of the notorious Auschwitz concentration camp in Poland.

My further acquaintance with the Hungarian Jews was not so pleasant; on the contrary, they will remain always one of my most unpleasant memories. When they filled my well-kept wards, it was not long before they had transformed them into pigsties. Neither persuasion nor threats could prevent them from answering the call of nature either in bed or on the floors, a thing that still could be forgiven if they had been seriously ill. But most of them were not, even if they were denied sulfonamides, the only medicine that could cure their erysipelas. This precious drug had become extremely rare during the last months of the war, and we had been instructed to give it only to the patients who were considered worthy of it — that these were always Communists and seldom others was understandable! Politics formed the main chapter of the medical handbook that was used in the hospital of Buchenwald!

At night the Hungarians sneaked through the ward to steal the bread of the others. There was a bloody fight if the thief was caught, and only my personal intervention could prevent murder. Even judging by the low moral standards of the average camp inhabitant, these Hungarians went beyond the boundaries of decency. Was it because they were Hungarian, or was it because they were Jews? I do not believe either. One thing one should not lose sight of: they all had gone through a period of misery and suffering that can never be described, and that would degenerate almost any man.

At any rate, they brought us near despair. Even Roland, a very quiet and sedate young man, and I myself, perhaps still more level-headed and unemotional, sometimes lost our patience with these people. Then was the first and only time I became guilty of slapping a patient, a practice I had always condemned with the other members of the hospital personnel, many of whom used to resort to this punishment as a daily routine. But I was forced to do it because it was the only thing that could make them obey. Many of them suffered from typhoid fever and dysentery, and it was my duty to do everything to prevent a possibly fatal epidemic.

In spite of the many sleepless nights that one of these, Jeno, caused Roland and me, his behavior, though tragic, was often most comic. The poor man had erysipelas of the face, which caused his eyelids to swell so that he was unable to see. At least that was what we thought. But one day when I guided him through the ward, while he had his hands searchingly stretched out in front of him, he suddenly stooped down to pick up a potato that was lying on the floor. He ate it peel and all. As he did not understand one word of German, I was unable to make him see how he had given himself away, and there was nothing else to do but to laugh about it. Gradually his intellectual faculties diminished, and he refused all food except the few apples I was able to get him. During the night he would suddenly jump onto the bed of his neighbor, who then in his fright would begin a wild struggle. We had hardly put him back to bed again, when he would climb upon the wooden beams that ran through the ward, and only with great difficulty could we get him down.

It was a great relief when he and all the others were transferred to a special barrack because there were too many of them to accommodate in my wards any longer. However, a few days before they left, I was called by Roland to the other ward. At that time I was in charge not only of my own ward but also of the neighboring one, as the former nurse, a young Russian, a jockey by profession and the son of a high functionary with the G.P.U., had been dismissed after a fight with one of the members of the camp police.

It was late afternoon; the lights were already on. Here I found a patient who had just arrived that afternoon, trying to end his life by strangling himself with a towel. His face was already greatly cyanotic, but when I loosened the towel he quickly regained his normal color. As he, like his blind countryman, did not understand German, I could not reason with him. I tied his hands together. About one hour later Roland called me again. I loosened the towel, and this time I tied his hands to a bed with a leather belt. I asked another Hungarian who spoke German well if he knew anything about this man. It appeared that he was a Hungarian who had been a member of the S.S. in his own country. He wanted to end his life, as he well knew that if he didn't, his fellow countrymen would kill him. This was his only escape.

Though I felt toward the Hungarian S.S. the same as I did toward the Nazis, which was far from friendly, I could not permit him to commit suicide in my ward. After all, he was my patient and as such I felt obliged to care for him without discrimination. I always considered this the only just course, even though my Dutch patients were disgruntled that I did not give them special advantages. So now, too, in spite of my contempt for this man, I wanted to treat him like any other sick man. Besides, I was convinced that once discharged from my care, he would get what was coming to him. But things happened faster than I could anticipate.

Back in my own ward, I was alarmed some time later by a tremendous turmoil in the neighboring ward. When I ran there, I saw to my horror this Hungarian S.S. man standing up in his bed while the other patients in deadly fear were assembled in the corner of the ward. Only now I noticed how strongly this man was built, and how well he was fed. No doubt he had not been in any other concentration camp before this, except perhaps as a guard.

He received me with a furious roar, his eyes full of hatred. He recognized the person who twice before had thwarted him in his attempt at suicide. With one mighty swing he pulled a heavy oak-wood locker from the wall and started for me. Quickly, Roland, who had followed me, and I succeeded in snatching the locker away, but the lid broke off and he still had a dangerous weapon in his hand. He made a dash for Roland, who ducked away. I told Roland to get a stick, as it was clear that the man had lost his senses and had to be disarmed before worse things would happen. Standing on his top bunk, the Hungarian looked around to see what or whom he could attack next.

Over the next bed a large, round glass lamp was hanging. Seeing this, the madman jumped onto the other bed just as Roland returned with a stick. I snatched it from his hands still in time to prevent the Hungarian from destroying the lamp. A wild duel began. For several minutes I was able to keep the wooden lid from hitting the lamp, but I realized that I could not do it much longer. I was in too unfavorable a position, though I was grateful for my training in fencing years ago. Suddenly the raving man changed his tactics; he raised the lid above his head to strike me with all his strength. I ducked and warded off the blow with the stick, but before I was able to recover, he struck at the lamp with a quick blow upward. The glass fragments shattered over my head. The room was now in darkness. Only light from outside illuminated faintly the scene of our struggle. He tore the iron stave by which the lamp had been suspended from the ceiling and broke it in two as if it were a straw. Fortunately, just then help came. Hermann, the Kapo, and several other nurses grabbed the madman by the legs, throwing him with a crash to the ground. A terrible struggle followed, but soon he was overpowered. The nurses dragged him to the bathroom, where he was placed under a cold shower. He still attempted several times to attack them, but finally fell down, dazed by the cold water.

Hermann was informed about the man's past history, and I left it to him and the others to decide what should be done with him. To bring him back into my ward was out of the question; to return him to his barrack in the quarantine camp would mean a well-earned death at the hands of his countrymen. Hermann's answer to this dilemma was to inject him with a solution of arsenic. Of course I disapproved of this, but did not feel any pity for a man who had betrayed his country in such a dishonorable way.

The end of this Hungarian S.S. man was in a certain way a favorable exception in the struggle for life, survival of the fittest, which usually ended with the death of helpless innocents, those who out of political or other motives had fallen into disgrace with the men in power. But here the fittest had been bested because he had placed himself outside the bond that united all prisoners regardless of race, nationality, religion, or political conviction — the bond of hatred and enmity toward Nazism.

❧ 24 ❦

There were about four hundred Dutchmen in the camp. Apart from the few who like me could be considered political refugees, and some escaped laborers, the Dutch prisoners were divided into two definite groups, the Orangists and the Communists. They were like water and fire. As the group of Dutch Communists was readily supported by the German Communists, the Orangists, or Royalists, were in a tough spot, although they ultimately came out relatively unharmed through their resolute and firm attitude.

From my friend Peter I learned even better several weeks after I had returned to Holland from Buchenwald how dangerous it was to be opposed by the Communists. Peter had been sentenced to death by a German court for espionage and the smuggling of American and English fliers over the Dutch border. Later his sentence was commuted to life imprisonment and he arrived in Buchenwald a few months after me.

"Koert," my friend said, "I still can hardly understand how you have come out alive from Buchenwald."

"Why," I replied, "every one of us had practically the same chance to die."

"Yes, but you are a Catholic and against everything Communistic." I interrupted him, "I knew only too well that the Communists were always intriguing against me, but I was very fortunate in being able to find good weapons against their hatred and dislike for me."

"Well, that may be so," replied my friend, "but there is something you do not know, because I never told you this before. Each of us had enough worries already as things were, and I did not want to increase yours by telling you what happened one day in the fall of 1944!"

I became curious and asked him to go on. "One day two Dutch nurses visited me to find out what I knew about you," he said. "I told them that I had had only the most pleasant experiences with you. Then they confided to me that they intended to get you out of the hospital and into one of the worst transports, as they did not think it just that a man like you, who had never used his hands for real human labor, should occupy such a privileged status in Buchenwald."

Greatly surprised at this news, I asked my friend the names of these two nurses, my own countrymen. When he told me, I could hardly believe it. One of them was the nurse who during the first months of my stay in the hospital had been very kind to me, lending me some papers or going out of his way to talk to me. It had been only later that I had found out that he had belonged to the Communist party, but as he showed himself to me always as a kind person, I never thought him to be capable of such a dirty trick. The camp slogan, "Trust no one" showed itself again true: trust no one, especially those who are very friendly!

Many of the prisoners, however, who could not find favor with the Communist clique, had to pay with their lives. Were it not for the sake of the truth, I would rather suppress the fact that there also existed Dutch Communists who were criminals. Yes, and they did not even hesitate to dispose of their political enemies either by sending them on a death transport or killing them directly by an injection of poison. Though I do not have the same convincing proof for this last method as I had for the deadly practices of Sulikov, at least my friends and I were quite sure that some of the Dutch Communists were doing treacherous work for their godless ideals.

That the Dutch Communists had a hand in making out the lists for the death transports was only too well known. Two of my friends who arrived at the same time with me from France found this out soon enough. They were my good friends Herman and Paul, the former Dutch consul at Perpignan in France. Upon their arrival in Buchenwald they both met several old friends from Holland, all belonging to the Royalists. These men secured them good jobs which they were to start on leaving the quarantine camp. One day all the members of our transport from France had been assembled outside the quarantine barracks where one by one we were asked our occupation by a German Communist, the chief of the labor office. Before it was our turn to answer, we learned that those who mentioned a profession not of any interest to the German war production, like that of law students, journalists, businessmen, and barbers, were placed aside for the transport. Those who said they were engineers, carpenters or plumbers, for instance, were allowed to return to their barracks.

Dolf, who was an engineer, and I advised our friends to lie and not to say that they were a consul and a student of economy, but they were so assured of the help of their Royalist friends that they refused, saying that I myself had been exempted from the transport to "Dora" the day before with the help of these same friends. They did not want to believe that it had been the S.S. doctor himself who had signed me off the transport list.

So my friends were put in the group that was to be sent on the transport. They were still optimistic, as they were certain that this would only be temporary, and that their friends would get them out of it without any trouble. But the influence of the Royalists did not save Herman and Paul. Many of these Royalists were excellent Catholics and had commanded respect from their fellow prisoners by their courageous behavior and honest attitude during the many years of their imprisonment. They had attained a certain power in the camp, but it was far from effective in comparison to that of the Communists.

The Dutch consul, while in the concentration camp of Compiegne, had made some unfavorable remarks about Communism, and a Dutch Communist in our convoy had reported his words to the German Communists in Buchenwald. No wonder all the efforts of the Royalists to get the consul out of the transport were in vain. The consul was a doomed man from the moment he entered the camp. Herman was pulled along in his wake as he was always in the company of the consul, and so was probably reputed to have committed the same crime.

Within six weeks Herman and Paul had been worked to death in "Dora." And so the ones who after a successful escape to England would have been rewarded by our Queen in a personal audience, were but condemned men in Communist-run Buchenwald. The same criminals who put them on the transport are now at large, holding official and important posts with the Dutch Communist party in the Netherlands!

The group of Dutch laborers, who had worked in German factories and machine halls, had been arrested when they had not returned to Germany after their leave, because they feared the constant American and English bombing of German territory. These laborers are only worth mentioning in so far as they were not an asset to the name of the Dutch, because of their character-less and undisciplined conduct during the months of their imprisonment.

I often wondered if the unfavorable reputation of some of the other nationalities was not caused in large part by the presence of a group like our escaped laborers and black marketeers. As a Dutchman it was easy for me to make a sharp distinction between the chaff and the wheat among my own countrymen, but to do the same in judging other nationalities was practically impossible. And what was clear for them, was not yet clear for others. That is why a generalized judgment of a group as a whole is extremely difficult if not impossible.

I have traveled enough in foreign countries to know that one can always find good, bad, and indifferent individuals anywhere one goes. Never, and certainly not in a community like a concentration camp, where only too often the worst character traits in men become manifest, never have I been inclined to consider a certain nation, a certain race, or a certain religious group contemptible or inferior because I had had an unpleasant or disagreeable experience with one or more of its representatives. Every nation, every race, every religious group has its good and bad members, so let no man say: "Lord, I thank you that I am not like one of them."

So discrimination and generalization did not find their

place in this book. When I have condemned Nazism and Communism, it was because their philosophies were bad and their methods even worse — this is too well known to warrant further discussion here.

I have tried to be impartial in my account of my experiences with Buchenwald's inmates, and with a variation on Mark Antony's funeral oration at the death of Caesar I want to say: "I showed you the camp's wounds, poor, poor dumb mouths, and let them speak for me."

Before I go on to the next chapter to describe the last days of Buchenwald, let me mention the 175 Allied fliers who arrived during the months of 1944. I lump them all together as the Allied fliers because, though they were of many different nationalities — Americans, English, Canadians, Australians and New Zealanders — they were one in their firm and brave attitude in the time of affliction. I do not know why they were brought into a concentration camp instead of to a prisoner of war camp. It could not have been because they were suspected of being spies. All Allied fliers who were caught in Nazi-occupied countries trying to escape after being shot down and who were without uniforms or other distinguishing marks, were either executed right away or, if shipped to this camp, hanged in the cellar of the crematorium.

But what did the Nazis care if they did not treat prisoners of war according to the Geneva Convention? So often they had disregarded and scorned it — in bombing Warsaw, Rotterdam, Coventry, and Budapest; in enslaving men, women, and children for their war industries; in ignoring the civil laws of the countries they had occupied — that one more offense against the Geneva Convention would not make any difference in their ultimate punishment.

It cannot be denied that for the Allied fliers, more than for anybody else, life in Buchenwald must have meant one of the most bitter disillusionments, a never-dreamt reality. The other prisoners had come from countries which already had been occupied for years and who in these years had experienced not only the horrors of a total war, but also the atrocities of the occupier. But our Western Allies had not gone through all these hardships; for them, this change of scene must have been nothing less than the transition from heaven to hell. But, in spite of this, I seldom heard them complain, not even those who spent their days lying sick in my ward.

Through the day, the fliers bivouacked in the open between the barracks on the dirty and muddy ground; at night they tried to find some sleep on the wood floors of the overcrowded barracks of the quarantine camp. They suffered much more from lack of food and a decent place to live than we, who had become gradually accustomed to these discomforts over the passing years.

I tried to spend all my free moments with them, as it was good to see these young men openly scorning the Nazis and the bad elements among the prisoners. On their faces were not the slavish resignation and submission which had gradually come over the bony faces of the other prisoners. It was good to see and to converse with men who had just arrived from a world where freedom was not an idle word and who expressed this freedom and the right to live their own way — so long denied to the enslaved people of Europe — so self-confident in their unconcealed contempt for their enemies. If ever there could have been a doubt as to the question of which side was fighting for a better world of peace, freedom and the natural rights of men, the sight of these courageous young people would soon have changed this doubt to a certainty. Neither Nazism nor any other form of dictatorship could ever offer to mankind the natural happiness and blessings which pertained to the governments of our Western Allies.

With them I enjoyed the good news that they soon were to be transferred to a prisoner of war camp, where a better, or at least no worse, life would await them, even if I were to miss their company so badly.

Though Martin Perkins, a young Englishman, did not belong to this group of fliers, the story of his captivity might well illustrate the bravery of all our Allied prisoners. I got to know him shortly after my arrival in the camp where he himself had been for a short time. He had been arrested in France where he had worked for the British Intelligence Service, as he had a fluent command of the French language. He confided in me that apart from the ordinary dangers which threatened us all, he did not feel quite at ease about the plans that the Nazis might have in store for him. At that time I did not know, of course, that he was a B.I.S. officer, so this idea of his appeared rather improbable to me. I tried to make him share my opinion that once in a concentration camp one could be sure that one's trial had been finished with entirely. To be in Buchenwald was the same as if one were actually dead and the records of dead men are forgotten, as dead men are no longer dangerous to their enemies. The more days, weeks, and months that passed, the more Martin began to believe I had been right. The Nazis had done nothing to confirm his feeling of uneasiness.

But shortly before our liberation, it became clear that his original suspicions had been correct. One day he was summoned to appear before the S.S. Commander of the camp. When he returned, he must have already known what terrible fate would await him. He was quieter than ever and mentioned his dark thoughts only to a Dutchman with whom he worked in the disinfecting building. The Dutchman told me his story later, as he knew that Martin and I were good friends. It was then too late to be of any help to Martin. It all happened too quickly.

When Martin had told his friend that he expected the worst, the Dutchman had at once advised him to get himself admitted to my ward, where after a few days he could have "died" officially, to start a new life with the prison number and the name of some prisoner who had actually died during his stay in my ward. This little trick had worked more than once. But Martin had refused this way out, as he did not want to endanger anybody else by his own dangerous position. Had I only had the time and the opportunity to convince him that the risk was small, and that nobody would have even hesitated to assist him, this story might have had a happier ending.

The next day after he had appeared before the Commander, the S.S. hung him in the cellar of the crematorium. It happened at three o'clock on Maundy Thursday of the year 1945. His last words to his friend had been, "Non, mon ami, pas au revoir, mais adieu!" ("No, my friend, not 'au revoir,' but 'adieu'!" "Au revoir" has the connotation of "until we meet again" while "adieu" has that of "farewell.") As a man he had lived, as a hero he had died! For him the day of liberation had arrived thirteen days earlier than for us.

≥ 25 ≤

The Nazis were retreating. It would be our last winter at Buchenwald. But this winter of 1944-45 would be a time of nightmarish remembrances for the survivors who saw the horrible suffering and dying of thousands of fellow prisoners. This was when the eastern concentration camps in Poland were being emptied into camps in Germany. The population before had been about twenty-five thousand; now with the evacuated prisoners, in spite of the thousands who had died on the way and the thousands who died after reaching the camp, that number was doubled.

It was a time of mass transportations, when the Germans were hysterically trying to eliminate their prisoners and abandon their prisons. These transports, which were used as a means of eliminating many thousands, were the most barbaric of all. During an eight-day foot march over frozen roads in temperatures far below freezing, the prisoners who could not go on were shot by their S.S. guards. These were the fortunate ones, for the living were put in open freight cars for the long bitter trip to Germany.

I saw those cars when they arrived at Buchenwald. I shall never forget it. Dead bodies were frozen together and to the sides and floors of the cars. The living were jammed in among the corpses. At my first horrible sight of this silent, human load, it looked as if all of the bodies would have to go to the crematorium, but after looking closely I could distinguish a few slight movements of some, and I knew there were still men living in that heap.

When these transports would arrive, all of the hospital workers, all of the members of the prisoner police force, and all of the corpse bearers would have to go out to the station to help unload. The corpse bearers then took away these freshly dead who had succumbed to the sudden change from the below-freezing temperature of the outdoors to the warm water of the showers. The bearers could not be blamed if some of the people they carried off were still alive. Their mistake was one of minutes.

In the quarantine barracks then, three men had to live in the space before allotted to one. The usually small food ration was cut in half. All the men who were hungry before, with the bones of their skulls pressing into their skin, now were starving, and they looked and acted like beasts who kill to live. These starving inmates of the quarantine camp would break into the hospital barracks at night to steal the food of the sick and the dying. Emaciated men strangled men even weaker than they in the barracks, and hid the bodies to receive their victims' rations. During the distribution of food, camp police had to keep order, for there was no discipline, and men were killing to get an extra crust for their stomachs.

There were many stories of cannibalism heard in the camp, but I saw thousands of cadavers and not one marred in such a way as to suggest such a thing. I did hear, though, of one prisoner, who was in a commando outside of Buchenwald, put in jail for exchanging a piece of human flesh for bread. Even before the arrival of the thousands of new prisoners, epidemics of typhoid fever could not be prevented, though they were checked in a short time. Every Saturday night, each prisoner was searched for lice by a nurse or a doctor. Those who had lice were immediately disinfected. Their clothes and blankets were given the same treatment. With the incoming transports, however, many more men did get the disease. The largest number of cases at one time in the camp was 175, which was surprisingly low considering the crowding of the prisoners in the barracks. The examinations were increased during these last months so that three times a week everyone was inspected to see if he harbored these creatures.

In the unheated barracks, five men slept under one blanket in cots which were stacked three high. Blankets were precious items, so the day two of them were stolen from the corridor of the emergency room, I was determined to get them back. They belonged to two of my patients who were being treated for some open wounds, and they had left the blankets in the hall as usual. The only clue I had to the theft was that two prisoners from quarantine barrack fifty-seven had brought one of their sick friends to the hospital. I went immediately to the barrack and asked the chief if he knew which men had gone to the hospital that morning. When I had told him the story, he replied sternly:

"Do you think one of my men could have done such a thing? That's impossible! No one here is a thief!"

I looked at him, amazed at his words.

"You probably want barrack sixty-three," he smiled cynically.

Then I understood him, and laughed with him. "Couldn't you tell your people that the blankets belonged to patients with scarlet fever? They'll want to be rid of them quickly enough then."

"We can try it." He motioned for men to come with him as he pushed his way through the swarm of men to the middle of the room where he climbed on a bench and blew his whistle. But there was no letup from the pandemonium caused by a thousand men. Again he blew the whistle, and then once more, but only the ones who stood close by stopped their talking and brawling long enough to see who was bothering them. Such disregard of authority would never have happened a year ago in those barracks. Discipline then had been strict and kept with a fist of iron.

Realizing it was hopeless to get any notice from the prisoners, I thanked the chief, and began to question each person as I came to him. I asked hundreds if they knew who had been taken to the hospital that morning. Finally, after a long search, I found out who it had been, and then it was easy to find his companions. Naturally they denied having the blankets, but when I took the men to the chief, a few threats on his part made them give up the stolen blankets.

I asked the chief not to punish them, because it had been my regulation that blankets be left in the corridor. It was a temptation almost too great for a saint to ignore two unaccompanied blankets if he had been sleeping night after night in a freezing barrack with but one blanket for himself and four of his bedfellows. I had nothing but compassion for these poor devils. I ordered them to carry their prizes back to the hospital, where I gave them some bread. How they wolfed it down!

If men had ever become beasts, it was during those last months before the liberation in the quarantine camp. The S.S. Commander thought little of man's dignity, or of the rights given man by God. It was for the Nazi and his kind to take away the freedom to use these rights.

Did the Commander of Buchenwald care that under the rule he represented men must live and die as animals? Did he care that in the quarantine camp fifteen hundred prisoners lived in barracks meant for five hundred? Did he care that the food rations had to be cut in half and later that meager portion was cut in half again? Did he care that the bacteria, the lice, and the fleas only had to cover the smallest imaginable distance from one victim to another? Why should he? These starving, sick, miserable skeletons were his enemies. And a Nazi did not pray for his enemies — or anyone else for that matter.

But the Commander of Buchenwald was happy. He had luxurious quarters and beautiful grounds around his spacious house. He had choice foods in abundance on his table. He made scrupulously sure that no bacilli parasitized on him. Yet will he remember some day the second inscription on the entrance gate of Buchenwald: "Jedem das Seine" (To each his own)?

❧ 26 ❦

During the last months before liberation, we lived no longer by the time of food distribution or the time of sleep but by the time of the news broadcasts. We listened in breathless silence to every word that came over the loudspeaker. Although the German radio never admitted a defeat, it was easy to know what advances the Allies were making by the names of the towns and cities that were mentioned. Even though the announcer talked only of German victories, he could not keep from naming ever more cities and villages closer to the German border. It was surprising that we were allowed to listen to the news at all. Every day now brought us some joy, for we could tell that the Allies were advancing and closing in on our captors.

There was not one prisoner who doubted that the Allies would be victorious, but we all had different opinions about the day victory would come. And though there were many pessimists who did not believe that the end was near, there were many more optimists. And that is understandable when one realizes that so often the wish is father to the thought. There were countless rumors circulating "from reliable sources" that the war would be over in a few weeks. Finally, to be sure of the truth, one did not believe any stories about the progress on the battlefields unless the German radio, which was always a few days late in recognizing German defeats, confirmed it. It went even so far that one of these optimistic prophets was promised a good beating if his prophecy did not come true. The man had to be hospitalized at the end of the predicted time to recover from his injuries!

If I remember well, it was the thirteenth of January, 1945, when I strained my ears to catch the words of the German announcer through the loudspeaker in my ward. The loud-

163

speaker was connected to a radio in the quarters of the S.S. and for some reason it did not work well that day. But I could hear well enough to learn that the Russians had renewed their offensive, and I could not withhold a cry of joy when I heard it. For months we had wondered why the Russian front, after having steadily moved forward from Stalingrad, had come to a halt just before Warsaw. We never had ways of learning about the political motives that played such an important role behind the scenes. But when the Russian armies had stopped their offensive, we knew that things were happening in the West.

One day the memorable news over our German radio proclaimed that our Western Allies had invaded France. Then Paris, the capital of France fell; Brussels, the capital of Belgium fell; the southern part of Holland below the large rivers was liberated. We were dazzled by the speed with which our friends advanced. If they could just keep it up!

On the sixteenth of December, 1944, we were disappointed but not discouraged about the Battle of the Bulge. We realized that this last, despairing gesture of the Germans would only hasten the final defeat of Hitler's armies. But we wondered why the Russians remained silent; without their strength in the war, this fight might last too long for us. Every day was valuable. The misery in our camp had reached its maximum; in every month of the year 1945 we counted five or six thousand deaths; in short, our position had become untenable.

Then the new Russian offensive started. Warsaw, where its underground army of thousands of heroic men and women had been destroyed in its futile wait for the promised Russian help, was liberated. Had the Communists halted their offensive deliberately so that the Poles were sure to die? Every day the German lines were rolled back many miles to the west as if no resistance existed.

On Tuesday, Herr Goebbels spoke of the faraway Russian goals like Silesia and Prussia — the next Friday the Russians had already arrived there. It was marvelous; we were continually making new maps as we charted the Russians' progress. The names of the cities in the news reports became more and more familiar. But despite the Allies' rapid advances, our uneasiness about our precarious condition grew by the day. We were still at the mercy of the S.S. Although we knew that the end of Nazi rule was not far off, we wondered if we would witness that wonderful day. We were glad for our relatives and friends at home who would soon see the dawn of freedom, for our respective fatherlands which already had been liberated from Nazi terror or soon would be, and we eagerly and trustingly looked forward to the approaching liberation of the whole world from Nazism, Fascism, and dictatorships of every stripe.

Was it not natural that now we too wanted to witness those happy days so near at hand? We had fought so long for this freedom and had suffered so many privations and so much misery in our struggle to regain it. Indeed, even now we would be ready as we always had been in the past to give our very lives for this goal of freedom. We would not hesitate to die like men if we must; but the wish to die — to make an end to our almost unbearable fate, a wish that at times during our most somber periods had won over faith in God and resignation to His holy will — was replaced by the wish to live now that the future appeared worth living for. For years and years the future had seemed so dark and terrible, like a night with no moon and no stars. Now not just a few points of light had appeared; even the largest part of the once pitch black sky had cleared up. It was a matter of months, or weeks — perhaps even days — when the whole sky would be clear and blue again. Though we were prepared to die until the last moment, we would fight as never before to see the defeat of the spirit of evil by the spirit of good.

That the danger we were in was greater than we expected would only too soon become evident. During the first days of April, the American armies had passed the boundaries of Thuringia, the province in the heart of Germany where our camp was situated. It was now apparent that we would be liberated by the Americans and not by the Russians. Gone was the hope of the Slavic prisoners that it would be the Russian army that would open the doors of our prison. We Westerners were happy that it would be the Americans. The Communist prisoners feared their just fate by the overseas armies whose democratic judgment could not be expected to appreciate or ignore their evil crimes. And so we Westerners, the declared enemies of Communism, were afraid that our imprisonment by the Nazis would be followed by imprisonment, if not death, by the Communists. Only our friends from overseas, and not the Red army, could secure our freedom.

But when we heard that in the province of Thuringia the resistance of the German army had become stronger, the nervous tension in the camp which had been mounting day by day became almost unbearable. Since the time that the bridge of Remagen over the Rhine had fallen unharmed into the hands of the American army, the Germans had been giving way. We knew that our Allies were in the neighborhood, but the Commander of Buchenwald knew this too. He began his extermination program.

Tuesday, April 3rd, 1945.

All German prisoners who held important jobs in the camp were ordered to assemble in the "Kino" hall, a huge barracks where on rare occasions German movies were held for the prisoners. It happened that several non-Germans, myself included, were ordered to be in the hall as well. When the S.S. Commander began speaking — the first time he had ever addressed the prisoners in the camp's long existence — we knew that the S.S. had not intended for some of us to be there. This was for German prisoners only!!!

The Commander started his dramatic speech about two o'clock.

"You all know naturally that the enemy is not far off and that in all probability he will reach Weimar in the next few days. It is my intention to surrender the camp to the Americans in the state it is in now. I do not contemplate any evacuation of the prisoners.

It is not that through this I want to save my own skin—that leaves me cold—but I have come here to warn you Germans. I want you all to come out of this place alive. After all, you are Germans and my countrymen, and I want to warn you that those dirty, foreign prisoners will try to kill you. I know that recently a German Kapo and another German commander of a commando which was evacuated from Duesseldorf to Buchenwald were killed on the night of their arrival. I have no doubt that this was done by those foreign swine. Thus you are warned. Take care that they don't get you, be ahead of them, and do not hesitate to exterminate them!"

Then he warned us about a radio emitter which he suspected was hidden in the camp. And then he called out, "Have you all understood me clearly?"

"Yes!" the prisoner gang thundered back to him.

Indeed, we had understood the meaning of his words only too clearly—especially we, the foreign swine. It was all too clear that he favored a general massacre among the prisoners which would do away with most of the foreigners and at the same time with some of his beloved countrymen, the German prisoners. But we also understood the great danger that lay ahead of us if there were to be a general evacuation. We had had too much experience with Nazi lies to rely on a Nazi promise. We knew now that the opposite of what the German Commander had told us would happen.

We were not worried about the German's advice to his countrymen. It was not likely that the German prisoners would turn on the foreign prisoners and slaughter them. It would be too much of an added risk to their own vulnerable lives. We prisoners were after all in this fight against the Nazis and S.S. together. In spite of the many national and political differences of the prisoners, we were one against our captor. But this peril of a general evacuation threatened us. We recognized the seriousness of this threat only too well from the transports that had arrived from Auschwitz, Maidanek, and other Polish camps with their dead loads. Those who had returned from their commandos in the western part of Germany had told us frightening stories about their suffering. They had been forced to flee before the Allied front without food or water and packed in closed cattle trucks. They had been driven on long foot marches and all those who were not able to walk quickly enough for the S.S. were shot along the road. Those who still had the strength to drag themselves forward were continuously endangered by bombardments and machine gunning from airplanes.

We in the camp were still entirely powerless and at the mercy of the S.S., even though lately the discipline had markedly lessened, and the prisoners got away with things which in earlier days would have been impossible.

Wednesday, April 4th, 1945.

The S.S. ordered forty-eight of the highly-positioned prisoners to appear before them. These prisoners were the leading personalities in the camp, like the Kapo of the hospital and the chief of the labor office. The S.S. were undoubtedly going to execute these men because they would be valuable witnesses to the Nazi crimes for the Allies. The names of the forty-eight had been given to the S.S. by a prisoner who had turned traitor and who had been released some time ago.

But discipline was obviously cracking, for none of these men appeared that morning at eight o'clock at the entrance gates of the camp where they had been ordered by their Nazi masters. These prominent prisoners shaved their heads — they were all exempt from the bald head rule — and put on some old clothes and some dead prisoner's numbers, and then they submerged themselves among the masses in the camp. In normal times, the regular roll-calls were so anxiously and preciously counted that this disappearance could never have been carried off. Now it was even worse. Many despondent unfortunates hid themselves beneath a barrack under the ground or in any place they could find. But when they were missing from the roll-call, every prisoner in the camp had to stand until the missing man was found, even if it took days to find him. These roll-calls were always very complicated procedures because of the numerous daily arrivals, the leaving transports, and the deaths. All prisoners had to stand at the place of roll-call until every name was called. Each roll-call was a tremendous ordeal and often cost many lives. So a missing person awaited only death — as either the S.S. or the prisoners were sure to make short work of him, the latter as they were put in serious jeopardy during the long exhausting wait exposed to the elements.

Now, however, when the death toll was sometimes two hundred or more a day, it was not possible to have an exact roll-call. The overfilling of the camp with the thousands who daily returned from the outside commandos added to the confusion. So there was a chance that the forty-eight hiding prisoners could remain undiscovered — for awhile at least. At any rate it was worth their trying, as the end of our imprisonment was not too far off. Every hour of life was gain and made the likelihood of salvation greater.

The camp police were ordered by the Commander to search the entire camp for the fugitives. But these prisoners were naturally on the side of the forty-eight, so they reported an unsuccessful search. Fortunately no reprisals were made. The S.S. had other and more important worries, for their time was running out. They must plan their method of exterminating all the prisoners, and thus also the forty-eight most dangerous ones. And they must do this before the arrival of the American troops.

Friday, April 6th, 1945.

Three days after the speech of the Commander, who had promised no evacuation, the evacuation of the Jews began. Those who had foolishly believed the Commander now despaired. That afternoon all prisoners of Jewish origin were summoned to appear at the entrance gates. The scenes that I saw that day were piteous. In endless rows the thin, feeble bodies hobbled up the

sloping muddy paths towards the entrance of the camp. The
Jews, resigned and stunned by long, long years in prisons and
concentration camps, had no fear. But the deadly certainty of the
fate that awaited them was written all over their dirty, emaciated
faces. Many of them fell down in the mud, some never got up
again, others lay there exhausted, and still others pretended to be
dead. Dusk fell and darkness came, and still all the Jews had not
reached the top of the camp. But they had waited for this. The
darkness was their ally. A wild panic began. Everybody — even
those who had been stretched out for hours in the mud like dead
— fled in all directions. They broke through the railing around the
hospital trying to find refuge in the wards. They listened to no
reason, and only force could prevent them from entering the
hospital. Finally the S.S. realized the hopelessness of getting them
together and ordered them to return to their blocks. The Jews had
gained a day and a night, but it would be of little avail as the
American forces did not come the next day.

Saturday, April 7th, 1945.

The S.S., having learned through their failure of the previous day, this morning sent several groups of S.S. men into the
camp. The S.S. men were unarmed, but they were impressive
enough to assemble a few thousand Jews in a few hours. Since for
many months the Jews had not worn yellow stars because of the
shortage of material, they had to be identified by their features,
including circumcision. Thus only a few Jews who missed the
distinguishing features of their race were able to escape the first
transport, of which no man was ever seen alive again.

There was one Polish Jew whom I unknowingly forced to
escape this first transport. For two months I had had his little son,
Janek, as a patient in my ward with scarlet fever. A cute little boy,
he was the youngest political prisoner in the camp. He was four
years old! By the time he had recovered from his illness, I had
become quite fond of the boy, who in his innocence and complete
ignorance of his misfortune was the sunshine in our gloomy

existence. I kept him under my care, for I thought it inadvisable to let him return to the filthy quarantine camp where his father was living. He was perfectly happy in my room, and I did my best to get him all the milk and extra food he needed.

On the day of the Jewish evacuation, his father came to get Janek to take him along on the transport.

In tears he urged me to give up his son, "My life is nothing without him," he sobbed. "His mother died in the gas chamber at Auschwitz. I have nothing left but my boy."

"Can't you understand how useless it would be for you to take him? He will only perish. I promise to keep him under my personal care, and I'll do anything to save him." I begged the father until he finally consented to leave Janek with me.

The poor man left the hospital crying bitterly, after a heartbreaking farewell to his son.

Great was my joy when on the day of liberation of Buchenwald, he came back to get his son. Unable to bear leaving Janek, the father had dug himself into the ground under one of the barracks, where he had stayed for four days and four nights. Knowing them both safe in their newly regained freedom, I happily returned the boy.

So the Jews had been led away, driven into death, and unable to resist. The only resistor was Kurt Baum, a German Jew, who in the night had found refuge in the cellar of the Dutch barrack, one of the few stone buildings in the camp. The next morning, however, he was discovered when the S.S. searched the entire camp for possible hideaways. Kurt succeeded in overpowering the S.S. officer and obtaining his gun, but before he was able to unfasten the safety pin, the officer attacked him again. In the ensuing struggle, the Jew was killed by the S.S. man. So Kurt died a more honorable death than the one he had destined for himself a year previously when he had been admitted to my ward after an unsuccessful attempt at suicide. At that time, it seemed totally unbelievable to me that someone who had been a prisoner of the Nazis since 1933 could give up when freedom was at last in sight.

Sunday, April 8th, 1945.

This drama, the evacuation of the Jews, took two days. There was still no sign of immediate help from outside. Fifty thousand men were in the greatest danger behind the barbed wire. Every one of us might soon share the fate of the unfortunate Jews. Waiting was agonizing. Then on this beautiful Sunday morning, a grating voice over the loudspeaker in the camp said that all prisoners were to appear at noon at the gates of the camp with a blanket and provisions for a few days. The sick, the hospital personnel, and the labor office workers were exempt from this order for the time being. Thus, at last!

Even knowing evacuation to be inevitable, I had not fully realized that it would materialize or that our approaching friends would not prevent it. But no, it seemed that the Commander still felt safe enough to carry into effect Herr Himmler's orders: "No prisoner in any concentration camp shall come out alive!" This was not a surprising statement. Nothing could be more logical than for the S.S. to destroy all compromising evidence, live or dead stock. And heaven and earth would be moved to destroy it.

So, that sunny spring morning in April, I wrote a farewell letter to my parents, brothers and sisters. I was dead calm. I tried to imagine how the end would come and what it would be like to die. Though I had never despaired of surviving the horrors of the concentration camp, I had forced myself to become familiar with the idea of dying here. Now that the end of my life seemed near, I could not help feeling amazed that I had no fear. Was I then already so little attached to life that I could part with it without sighs or tears? The grief and misery of thousands around me had not failed to leave their trace upon my soul. Never had I seen one of my fellow prisoners die with tears in their eyes or with a cry to save their lives upon their lips. Soft and calm, unnaturally quiet, their lives drifted away. At times I had had to resist a feeling of envy for the dead who were freed so easily from this monstrous hell on earth.

The only thing that always worried me was the uncertainty

about the fate of my dear ones at home. Lately we had heard that the people in Holland, who were still under the yoke of the Nazis, suffered under the direst and most bitter privations. Starvation, inundation, poverty, and oppression had made our little country, once so prosperous in every respect, one of the most pitiful places in Europe. Yes, I may say that I would have had hardly any cares or fears if I had been in the world by myself without relatives. One accepts so easily circumstances which one before would have thought to be unable to bear. One resigns oneself so easily to the inevitable — be it hunger, thirst, cold, poverty, or the danger of dying. But I was tortured by the thought that perhaps one of my family might have known the suffering I had known, and it was that constant fear that made life in Buchenwald so doubly hard. How much more painful is mental anguish than physical hurt! There was no fear for personal danger, though this resignation to fate did not mean that one had to be a cowardly fatalist devoid of the will to live. This will was always present, and now with death so near it burned fiercer than ever, even if it was only to cheat the Nazis of their devilish intentions. And so these and other thoughts went through my mind that morning as I tried to understand my feelings.

I wrote my parents not to cry over me as God had been so good to be with me constantly under the form of bread, and that I was going to die in His Grace, given over to His holy will. I finished my letter and put it inside my clothes. If any American soldier found it on my body, he would send it on to my family, I trusted.

The hands of the clock slowly advanced to the hour of twelve. The lower parts of the camp became more and more crowded while the huge roll-call place near the entrance gate was entirely deserted. It was evident that not one person was going to obey the orders of the S.S. A frightened silence came over the crowd of prisoners when noon came. The S.S. Commander himself entered the camp and in one of the barracks he stood with his gun in his hand and ordered all of the prisoners there to go to the gates. Instead they jumped out of the windows and fled in opposite directions from the gate. The camp chief, one of the German Communists, then was asked why the prisoners refused to be evacuated. The Commander was told that they were afraid of the bombings and machine-gunnings by the Allied planes of the trains, as many of those who had recently returned from outside commandos had gone through this nightmare.

The Commander returned to his office and ordered all official interpreters to report there. None of them obeyed, so the second order to evacuate was broadcast in the German language only. When again there was no response, the Commander employed a different tactic. The prisoners were now coaxed with friendly promises, but friendliness from the S.S. was always distrusted and nobody fell for it. The situation became more critical by the minute as reprisals would soon be the Nazis' next move.

At two o'clock, when the sun in the bright sky threw hardly any shadows, a group of four hundred heavily armed S.S. men entered through the camp gates and dispersed over the camp. Four hundred against fifty thousand, it was an uneven match, but then the prisoners had the disadvantage. Within half an hour all prisoners had been driven together to the roll-call place; only those who had been killed by the wildly shooting S.S. bandits were missing.

Our passive resistance, unparalleled in the history of Buchenwald, had been broken. Further resistance would have meant immediate death; now there was still life, and thus still hope, however little.

Ten thousand prisoners were evacuated that same day and were started on a journey which only death would terminate. The darkness for which everyone had longed brought some relief from the terrific tension of that day. We knew we could not be sent out during the night. Our anxiety was great. Where were our American friends? Not a single plane had been observed that day, while previously, when the Western front was still far away, they could be heard and seen day and night. What did it help us now to remember the terrific night raids on Leipzig and other towns, whose blazing fires brightened the night sky for miles around? The thunder of the exploding bombs had been like music in our ears, but now when an air-raid alarm could have interrupted the mass evacuation, no humming sound of approaching airplanes, nor the sinister yet pleasant wail of sirens, could be heard by the inmates of our doomed camp.

Yet our rescue was not too far off and, though unknown to us at that time, it was brought about from within the camp itself. That Sunday a long-time Austrian prisoner escaped with the help of an S.S. man, got a motorbike and made it to the American lines. He told the Americans of the extremely precarious position of the prisoners in Buchenwald and implored them to do everything to liberate them in the quickest possible way. General Patton, then, whose strategic plans could not be expected to reckon with a non-military object such as Buchenwald, must have decided to change his plans in order to relieve the camp by a quick advance.

However, I want to emphasize, that I never heard this incident being officially confirmed, though later after our liberation, when I worked as a sworn-in interpreter with the Judge Advocate Section under Lt. Colonel Raymond Givens and with the Criminal Investigation Board under Major Purroy E. Thompson, I heard about an arrested S.S. man in the prison of Weimar who wanted to make a statement in his own favor in connection with the escape of one of the prisoners. This incident of our hastened rescue might thus be called very probable, but I wanted to stress this point that, in case it might not have been true, this story would not be derogatory to the truthfulness of other and perhaps more unbelievable happenings mentioned in this book, the truth of which I can vouch for fully.

Monday, April 9th, 1945.

This new morning came bringing no new sign of liberation. We were still in the perilous position of the night before. Further resistance by the prisoners against the evacuation was impossible. Only the American Army could save us now from certain death. Every hour, yes, every minute might be the difference between life and death and with that in mind every prisoner dragged out the S.S. orders as much as he dared. Our meager food rations were distributed much too late or not at all. The Commander was asked to wait a few hours with the evacuation as the men could not leave without having something in their stomachs or before having received their three days' provisions.

But in spite of all our purposeful delays that Monday, another ten thousand of us were evacuated. At least that was an improvement over the day before when the same number of evacuees had taken half a day to be organized for shipment. Now the whole day had been used. In the evening we who remained in the camp became optimistic when we observed the flashes of gunfire to our northeast. It seemed that the Americans were engaged in an encircling movement towards Weimar, so that the road of our transports might be expected to be cut off within the next few days.

Tuesday, April 10th, 1945.

That night, like the last two nights, brought some relief from the day's apprehension. But again the old fear returned with the new dawn. That day another nine thousand prisoners left the camp, and towards evening the total number that had been evacuated had reached twenty-nine thousand. We later heard that only an extremely small percentage of the men in these transports lived. Most of them were killed, and many were already shot before they reached Weimar, five miles from our camp, as they were unable to keep up with the march tempo. Some groups were entirely exterminated by machine guns or flame-throwers, and so effectively that several of the S.S. guards were victims of their own slaughter!

Five thousand prisoners were put into fifty cattle trucks which went on to the concentration camp of Dachau near Munich in Bavaria. Not one body was found alive when these trucks were discovered by the Americans not far from Dachau. Twenty days — pressed together in narrow cattle trucks, without water, without food, without fresh air, the atmosphere infected with perspiration and other excretions, crying, yelling, fighting, raving mad men, murder, manslaughter, suicide, and a steadily increasing heap of cadavers! And then silence... See there a story that not even a Sax Rohmer could have depicted in his wildest fantasies!

Twenty-one thousand prisoners still remained in the camp. Perhaps some of them would be there to welcome the U.S. Army. Tuesday afternoon, all members of the hospital staff were summoned together for a meeting. Only those few who had accompanied their friends who had been selected for evacuation were missing. We were all given the choice of remaining in the camp or of joining our friends who had to leave. For me the choice had not been difficult; for almost a year and a half, hundreds of patients had been trusted to my care and in my position in the hospital I had enjoyed many privileges. I could not leave them helpless now. No, I would stay on my post until the last, even though many tried to persuade me to leave the camp as they thought this would offer a better opportunity to escape. Moreover, my physical health was not too good; a generalized edema especially of head and extremities had gradually developed, and even a short walk up the gradual sloping paths of the camp would bring on shortness of breath and a quickening of the heart. In such a condition I did not think I had the stamina to escape from a well-guarded transport. So I would either become one of the victims of the Nazi extermination plans, or one of those liberated by the Third United States Army.

The top men among the hospital staff members decided that afternoon to submit a petition to the S.S. Commander to leave the invalids in the quarantine camp and the sick with the hospital personnel in the camp under the protection of twenty S.S. guards. The signers of the petition would guarantee fully the safety of these soldiers upon liberation. Among the signers were Professor Charles Richet of the Sorbonne, Henry Crooks, functionary with

the American consulate in Brussels and Lyon, a high French
Army officer, a Polish prince, two English journalists, and representatives of all other nations. Would it be any use? It seemed
extremely improbable, but it had to be tried as the sick and the
invalids would never survive even a decent transport.

If the Commander, who fled that very night to safer places,
had received this petition, how ironically would he have laughed
when he read our entreaty. Of course he would permit us to stay.
He never even thought of evacuating these cripples; for them
there awaited a very special surprise!

The Commander of "Nora," the nearest airfield, had been
ordered to bomb and destroy the entire camp with all the remaining inmates! He had refused. Were there no more planes or did he
fear enemy reprisals? At any rate it would not have been humani-
tarian feelings which prompted him to disobey this order.

The Commander's extermination program was further de-
tailed. Gas was to be used to kill those who escaped the bombardment. If this was ineffective, no worry, a special regiment of
soldiers was already on its way to complete the extermination.
This regiment had been formed in the course of the years by
former prisoners, mostly criminals, who had been left the choice
to fight in this special regiment on the dangerous Russian front or
to stay in the camps and in the prisons where they had been for
years. Fortunately for us, this group of professional criminals was
cut off at the last minute by the advancing Americans and so
prevented from executing their diabolical orders. Himmler's
plan to destroy all evidence had been well-prepared. However,
execution of the plan would never be carried out.

Wednesday, April 11th, 1945.

Was there a soul in the camp who suspected what an
important day this was going to be? That on this day the first of
the Nazi concentration camps would fall into the hands of the
enemy intact, so that the whole civilized world would receive the

irrefutable evidence of the murders of Hitler's highly praised "Nazi culture"? That on this day prisoners would see the end of imprisonments ranging from a few months to twelve years in length?

No, I do not believe there existed one prisoner who, though hoping it most ardently, dared to imagine it. On that beautiful spring day the tears, not now of despair and misery, but of happiness and gratitude, came into the eyes of the twenty-one thousand survivors who had expected death on the threshold of the world's new freedom.

This day at noon, the next group of ten thousand men were to report for evacuation. At exactly five minutes to twelve the new S.S. siren which had recently been installed in order to warn the Nazis of the approaching enemy, howled. Though it had been tried only once, we recognized the beautiful, unforgettable, and sinister sound immediately. The siren seemed to scream "freedom" to us. But we stood stunned at knowing that what we had waited for so long was really ours. Twenty-one thousand of us had lived to breathe again, but fifty-one thousand lay quietly, indifferent to the sound. They had starved, thirsted, suffered tortures, diseases, suffocation, and beatings. They had already had their call to freedom.

We saw American tanks approach in the distance. We heard the rattling of the machine guns. The S.S. men left the watch towers around the camp. The prisoners obeyed the last S.S. order to stay inside their barracks, but only to dig up from under the ground the guns and ammunition, which over the years had been stolen from the S.S. factories. For hours in past days, the prisoners had stood in rain, snow, and cold waiting while the S.S. searched the camp for these very weapons.

The electric current on the barbed wire around the camp was disconnected, and the wires were cut with large pliers. The Communists emerged in secretly trained groups and with their guns started to pursue the fleeing S.S. men. Others remained in camp to "maintain order" as they called it, but in reality to protect themselves from their opponents among the prisoners.

At four o'clock, the white flags were hoisted from the roofs of the barracks as a sign that the concentration camp of Buchenwald as such had ceased to exist. The United States Third Army under the great General Patton had arrived in the nick of time! God bless them!

The crematorium had burned its victims for the last time; never again would the flames escape from its chimney to set the blackness of the night aglow; never again would the S.S. give reign to its sadistic passions in the torture rooms underneath the crematorium; the experiments with the typhus virus on power-less victims were at an end. The Communists had lost their protective cloaks under which their terror and crimes had found such a fearful soil; the hunger had lost its fear; death had to loosen its mighty grip; the evil had been defeated, the good and God had triumphed.

❧ 27 ❧

Just after four o'clock on liberation day — three hours after the arrival of the Americans — the telephone rang in the office of the S.S. Commander who had cleared out long before. One of the German ex-prisoners answered it. The voice over the receiver said: "This is Schmidt, the chief of police in Weimar; I want to talk to the Commander."

The former German prisoner replied that the Commander was not in his office and asked the chief of police to call again in a half hour as the Commander might be back by then.

"All right," Schmidt answered, "I'll ring again." By this time there was not an S.S. man in the camp except for those who were in hiding among the prisoners, which they were able to do by shaving their heads and putting on the striped prisoner uniforms. The latter they had cherished for this purpose. As far back as August 1944 — the time of the air raid — we had seen prisoner uniforms in the burned S.S. barracks!

After about thirty minutes the telephone rang again. It was Herr Schmidt. Then the telephone conversation, as told to us by the Kapo of the main hospital, went like this:

"Could I now talk to the Commander?" asked Herr Schmidt from Weimar.

"Sorry, but the Commander hasn't returned yet; perhaps I could give him a message for you?"

"Well, I only wanted to know how things are in the camp. Is everything quiet?"

"Yes, everything is comparatively quiet."

"Are the guards still on their posts around the camp?"

"Certainly, all the watch towers are occupied." He did not

181

add that they now were occupied by former prisoners who were looking out for hiding S.S. men!

"Have all the prisoners been killed yet?" Herr Schmidt asked.

"No, not all, about half of them have been taken care of."

"Well, tell the Commander that he'd better be sure that they are all killed before dark tonight. The American forces are almost here, and if those swine would get free, unpleasant things might happen here in Weimar!" Herr Schmidt hung up.

Once more the Nazi system had shown its vile and immoral face, but for us at least it had been the last time. We would suffer no more from it. The chief of police was afraid that the prisoners escaped from the unlocked gate of Himmler's infernal institution would cool their wrath on the people of Weimar, the nearest town. And, indeed, I would not have been surprised if there had been violence and murder. Surely, these thousands of men — birds of all feathers — who had suffered the long years of hardships, privations and tortures in their imprisonment might react with ferocious hatred and the desire to kill.

Therefore I was not a little amazed when I saw the first captured S.S. men being returned to the camp while the former prisoners watched in baleful silence. Yet no hand was stretched out to lynch these Nazis; only an occasional, abusive word was thrown at them. Did no glowing hatred against our torturers burn in our breasts? Had that hatred suddenly been extinguished? No, that would take a long time. My own feeling of contempt was too vivid. I was afraid and ashamed of myself that I could hate so intensely. What a poor Christian I still was that I could not live up to God's command to love my enemies!

But I could not take justice and retaliation into my own hands. I knew that those criminals would be rightly judged and sentenced, and that no one would escape punishment. But could I expect this same self-control from the thousands of other Nazi victims, men who in all probability had endured more hardships than I, men who were more passionate than I, and men who were used to following instantly their inflamed passions?

No, I am sure that their hatred was even greater than mine, but I am inclined to think that they had not yet been able to free themselves from the slavish submission and fear that the S.S. had instilled in them over their prison years. They could not realize yet that now they were the masters and the S.S. were the captives.

Though this must certainly have been the most important reason why the freed prisoners did not at once turn in revenge on their cruel enslavers, as far as the Germans among them were concerned, I gradually got the feeling that these men were already making excuses for the German atrocities, "These Nazis were merely human beings — they were forced to do the beastly things they did!"

A few days after our liberation, some German soldiers and S.S. men wearing Red Cross armlets were sent to our camp to learn to work as nurses in the hospital. The camp was to be used for captured Nazis and S.S. men as soon as the former prisoners were returned to their homes. The Belgian and French prisoners were returned to their countries soon after liberation, but the Dutch had to wait more than a month before arrangements were made for their return. So I was still in my ward with only two patients left when the captured Germans began to arrive.

One Sunday morning I awoke to find a German soldier in my nearly empty ward. I rubbed my eyes to see if I was not dreaming, but the uniform and the cap did not disappear.

"What are you doing in my ward?" I asked the man.

"I was sent here to learn how to nurse the sick," he said.

"Oh, very interesting. Start with taking off your cap," I ordered.

The cap came off. "Good," I said, "Now go and scrub the whole ward."

"But I have come to learn nursing, not to clean floors," he answered back.

I became angry. "As long as I am here in this ward you will not touch one of my patients. A few days ago the idea of caring for a prisoner at the point of death would not have occurred to you. Start scrubbing, and quick!"

I turned over in my bed and grinned at my two remaining patients, who like me were feeling sweet revenge. Half an hour later the former soldier came to ask me in an irritatingly submissive manner, so typical of the characterless way the Germans responded to their defeat, what he should do next.

"The corridor, the washroom, and the toilets," I replied.

As several S.S. men who still were at large had destroyed the pumps which provided the camp with water, the would-be nurse would have a job just hauling water. Those rooms in the hospital had become filthy, and I knew it would take him a long time to clean them. I wanted to sleep a little longer as I enjoyed the luxury of unlimited bed rest, a thing unknown in former Buchenwald days.

When I awoke, the soldier had finished scrubbing, and I ordered him to polish my shoes. "And if I see one spot on them, then..." I got my old, worn-out shoes back looking like new. Polishing boots is a very important point in the training of German soldiers!

"For the time being," I told the man, "I do not want to see you anymore. When I need you, I'll call for you."

That afternoon I found five of these creatures in my ward busy making beds. "What is the meaning of this?" I demanded.

"We are to sleep here," one of them answered matter-of-factly.

"Sleep here?" I was incredulous. "Who told you that?"

"The Kapo."

"That's out of the question!" I bellowed. "I do not want to sleep under the same roof with your kind. Get out of my room."

Seething with rage, I went to see the Kapo about this tactless way of arranging things. As he was not in his room, I talked with his temporary substitute, the Czech surgeon, the same one who had so often intrigued against me. I took the opportunity to tell him what I thought of him and of the way he had toadied to the Communists. The arrival of a few ladies of the American Red Cross prevented me from going at him. As he had refused to provide beds for the German soldiers elsewhere, I went to the other nurses of my barrack, all German Communists, and told them that I would leave that same evening for the Dutch barrack if those soldiers were to remain in my ward. They finally consented to put the Nazis in another ward, but not without remarking, "How implacable are those foreigners."

These men who spoke had fought and suffered for twelve years under a regime that has yet to find its equal in perniciousness, in violation of rights, and in practices unworthy of men, and if they had already begun to take such an attitude, then I saw a gloomy future ahead and the forerunner of a repetition of 1918.

Not that we should not forgive. We pray that every day: "Forgive us. . . as we forgive those who trespass against us." And we should mean these words. But at the same time we are right and just if we do not want the culprits to escape punishment, so that they will be kept from persevering in their evil deeds.

Often I have been asked to explain how human beings could degenerate so much that they were able to commit such fiendish crimes. Conceited as I was in trying to appear as an intelligent man, I tried to answer this question with big words — sadism, inferiority/superiority complexes, mass suggestion, and so on. None of these words touches the core of the problem. There is only one answer, very simple in itself, but not always liked or appreciated by those who ask. *Evil flourishes because people no longer obey the laws and commands of God.* They no longer prayed and had put man and his finite intellect above God. It is a simple answer, but contemplate it and you will recognize its irrevocable truth. No one who lives in the grace of God COULD EVER commit such atrocities as this last war has seen.

Indeed it is a terrible truth and one which, at the same time, holds the solution to the future. We cannot live in peace, we cannot stay away from another war unless we return humbly to God and live as He wants us to live. There may be huge economic, political, and social problems that confront the world today which, if not solved, will greatly endanger the peace, or rather the present state of not having an actual war. But all these problems are miniscule compared to that enormous problem of how to bring men and women back to God.

One of the French priests imprisoned in the concentration camp of Buchenwald once said, "When one speaks of the privilege to have come out alive from Buchenwald, one also should consider the fact that it has been a greater privilege to have been sent there, and even this, without the first, is a privilege indeed."

Yes, it has been a privilege, even though in the beginning I rebelled against God's holy will, and in my conceit demanded an answer as to why it had to be me and not my neighbor who had to undergo such misery. But as time passed, my eyes were opened, and I began to see what before I could not comprehend. I had come to understand the real value of the things that I had once thought important and worth living for. When life was sweet and carefree, I had valued money, for example, because I thought it could buy me happiness; it could not, however, buy me freedom. The best of foods and wines and all the delicacies that please the tongue had also once seemed important, yet bread and water sufficed to keep body and soul together. I valued a carefree life, reaping the fruits of my education; however the miseries of prison life had taught me the real meaning of life. I had not valued God and His commands, but now in prison I realized that I could not live without Him — that life without God has no meaning.

Buchenwald was a hard and bitter experience, but it was an advantage to those who knew how to profit from it. Why does God permit wars and concentration camps? Again the answer is simple: because He loves us, because He wants to bring back to His fold those who otherwise in a life of pleasure and lusts would have been lost.

But there are still too many people in this world for whom this last war has not brought the answer to the meaning of life. The frightening number of divorces, criminal abortions, murders and other crimes in our present time prove this only too well. But God takes care of those who believe in Him and are called according to His purpose — even in the face of tragedy, for they are all His children. Unfortunately, however, the present generation too may have to learn this lesson the hard way as we did in Buchenwald unless they wake up soon. For them World War III is always looming on the horizon with its threat of atomic anhiliation. Will the present generation wait to see the hand of God reaching for them in another horrible war before they turn back to Him in prayer? Let us hope not, for then it may well be too late.

Lest we forget!

PART TWO

28

It was a cold evening in October 1946 when I met the girl I was later to marry. It was an unusual and yet conventional meeting. She and her parents lived in Evanston, Illinois at the time and I was working at Loretto Hospital in Oak Park, Illinois. I met Reverend Mother Eleanor Regan of the Sacred Heart convent at Lake Forest, Illinois when I called as a courtesy to nuns of the same order as those who had in Europe taught my mother and sister. I had been touring the Chicago area with a friend, when I saw the sign "Barat College." Since the foundress of the Sacred Heart Congregation was St. Madeleine Sophie Barat, I asked if these were the Mesdames of the Sacred Heart. My friend nodded, so I inquired if we might call at the convent. It was a touch of home for me. Anyway, I met Mother Regan, and she was very cordial. She was also a matchmaker!

She called her sister, Mrs. Thomas Kennedy, to tell her of my Sacred Heart connection. Mrs. Kennedy then wrote me a note to ask if I could come for dinner on a Sunday. I was happy to accept, and so I met Mary Jean, who was to become my wife. I don't remember thinking she was the one for me, and she felt the same, she told me later. I did think she was pretty!

It was not hard to make conversation with the Kennedys. They were fascinated with the stories I told about the war and my experiences. Sometime during the conversation it came up that Mary Jean's birthday was January 1, and I told them that mine was January 2! What a coincidence! They then asked me over for New Year's Day, 1947, to celebrate the birthdays. After that I was not in touch with them again. I was a resident at Loretto Hospital in Oak Park and did not have much time off.

In June, I heard by postcard from Mary Jean, who was

travelling in California. Encouraged by this sign of friendliness, I telephoned and asked her out after she returned to Chicago. At that time the dates involved me coming all the way into Chicago on the elevated train from Oak Park, transferring to the Evanston Express, and coming to pick Mary Jean up (which took about two hours). We would go into Chicago — once we saw "Annie Get Your Gun" with Mary Martin — for dinner and a show or movie. Then I brought her home.

All of this took me a good six hours. As we dated, I liked her more and more. I began to tell her about my father, whom I loved very much, and who had died three weeks before I came that night the previous fall for dinner. At the time I was so distraught — there was no one in Chicago, of course, who had known my father — that without thinking I boarded a train for Toronto, Canada, where a good friend of mine, Marinus Janssen, from Holland, lived. I spent a few days there and returned by train. Luckily no one asked me for my passport or visa, for I would have been in deep trouble if they had. Perhaps this story would have been very different!

I remember Mary Jean trying to tease me to cheer me up — I was so serious (with such a background, who wouldn't be?) — and she told me what a wonderful smile I had; it lit up my whole face. I gradually told more about myself — the things you have read about at the beginning of this story. Following the liberation, I spent three months in Germany translating for the Americans and then I returned home. In 1943, when I joined the underground, I was just short of my medical degree. That accomplished in the summer of 1945, I looked forward to coming to the United States, but since the quota had been scrapped during the war, I applied for a student visa, since a group called the World Student Service wanted me to make a tour of the United States to tell of my war experiences. My chance came when a friend told me — with one day's notice — that there was a berth on a ship leaving Jan. 3, 1946. I had little time to think, but decided to go.

I had celebrated my birthday with my family the day before. Parting from my father was especially poignant. He had been very ill after a stroke early in the war years. I knew I could not easily return once I was in the U.S., and realized I might never see my father again. As has already been mentioned, my father died in October 1946.

The trip across the Atlantic took 18 days because of a violent storm which slowed the passage and left most of the crew and passengers ill. I spent the time playing bridge with anybody who could sit up. Luckily, I did not become seasick!

I brought with me a small business card which l was to give a certain family in Washington, D.C. if I reached there: "Take care of my dear son Koert," signed, with a shaky hand, "Walter F.C. Baars." I kept this card with all the treasured memories of my past.

So I arrived in the U.S. and was taken under the wing of the World Student Service Fund, a body sponsored by the United Student Christian Council in the U.S.A., Student Service of America, Inc., and B'nai B'rith Foundations at American Universities, and began my tour of the U.S. The tour took me from New York to St. Louis, Missouri, and thereafter to Texas, where I talked in Dallas, Fort Worth, Nacogdoches, Austin, and San Antonio; the Midwest, including Kansas City, Missouri; Omaha and Kearney, Nebraska; Chicago, Illinois; Indianapolis, Indiana, and Cincinnati, Ohio; and finally back again to New York City.

About April 1946 I managed to find a spot at a Mount Vernon, N.Y. hospital as an intern. Eventually I moved to Chicago and became a resident at Loretto Hospital, Oak Park, Illinois. My good friends there were George Wickster, M.D., head of OB/GYN, and Herbert Ratner, M.D., who later became public health officer in Oak Park and now is very active in pro-life writing and the National Catholic Physicians Guild. One of my fellow residents was Marian Primomo, M.D., a native of San Antonio, who discovered in 1979 that we were in San Antonio and welcomed us warmly. She and I had lost contact completely in the intervening years.

At any rate, I met Mary Jean at that point in my life and we dated quite often in the fall of 1947. She told me much later that she mentioned to one of her co-workers that I was the kind of man she would like to marry. We were not in love then — or if so, had not acknowledged it even to ourselves. She had given no sign of an interest more than friendship. She blushed, though, when in answer to her remark about how pretty some blonde dancers were in a show we were watching, I looked at her intently and said, "Brunettes are pretty, too!"

New Year's Eve, 1947, came around and I had asked Mary Jean to go to someone's house for a celebration to see the New Year in. We finally left the party about 3:00 a.m. and somehow or other there we were, acknowledging our love and talking about marriage.

We stopped at a church for the 4:00 a.m. Mass — incidentally, by this time I had acquired my first car, a 1940 Buick which even had a searchlight on it — and then I took her home. It was a misty, rainy, and later icy night as so often happens when the old year ends in Chicago. The driving was treacherous and it kept getting foggier. Mary Jean was worried that I had to drive all the way back to Oak Park. It was nice to have somebody concerned about me! When we reached her home in Evanston, we bid each other an affectionate goodnight, and I left.

Twenty minutes later I returned asking if the Kennedys could put me up, the conditions were so bad: ice and heavy fog. They had a pull-down bed in the living room, so they kindly got it ready for me. Then we all turned in for the night. I was quite excited to be under the same roof as M.J.!

I really don't remember celebrating our birthdays together, though I'm sure we did. The next thing I remember is the death of Mary Jean's grandmother in February 1948. Her mother went up to Minneapolis for the funeral, and the next weekend I called Mary Jean from Loretto Hospital, where I was in bed recovering from the flu. I asked her to come out, because I had something to tell her. I was going to ask her to marry me. She told me later that she was pretty sure it was a marriage proposal, so she told her father all about it, and that she thought she was going to say yes.

There was a lot of time on the elevated to think about it — it was a two hour ride.

When she came into my room, I could see from her face that her answer was yes. We decided that if possible we would be married right after Easter, as my visa was due to expire then and I could apply for citizenship as the spouse of an American.

❧ 29 ❧

The next month is a blur in my memory except for a few details. We went to St. Mary's Church in Evanston to make arrangements for April 3, Easter Saturday, at the 11:00 a.m. Mass; the earlier times were already scheduled for other weddings.

In those days there were no afternoon or evening Masses. Mary Jean and family decided on a very simple wedding — she decided to be married in a suit and hold only a wedding breakfast for the wedding party and relatives. Both she and I were given instructions on marriage by Fr. Paul McArdle, first together, then separately. I remember Father's instructions were profound in the wisdom of the Church in her care of us, her children.

Mary Jean's friends at the office gave her a shower at the home of her uncle and aunt. Finally the day arrived, a beautiful sunny and cool April day. The Kennedy family went to early Mass and Communion, since 11:00 was very late to fast — the fast was from midnight then — and I went to early Mass and Communion at Loretto Hospital's chapel.

M.J.'s parents rented a car for the day as we were going to the Orrington Hotel for breakfast after the Mass. I don't remember too well the ceremony and the Mass except for the beautiful vows as we repeated them, "to have and to hold, from this day forward, for better, for worse, for richer, for poorer, in sickness and in health, until death do us part." Our wedding book of candid photos tells more than I can write.

As with all people, it was a day for memories. I always claimed, laughing, that I never remembered a thing. Husbands have a way of claiming this! I had been sick in the hospital for three days prior to the wedding, and could not be at the rehearsal.

Neither could my best man, George Wickster, who had been delivering a baby Friday night!

At the Orrington, my family from Holland made us a long distance call. I have not cried much in my life, but I did that day, and Mary Jean hugged me and tried to comfort me. Would that Mother and the others could have been there.

❧ *30* ❧

The first year of our married life was pretty eventful. After a honeymoon in the Smoky Mountains of Tennessee we found an efficiency apartment in north Chicago and spent some time cleaning it up. It was pretty sooty from the Chicago atmosphere. It had a Murphy bed, a bed which was stored in the wall and pulled down at night.

M.J. kept her job as a secretary, and I continued as a resident at Loretto Hospital. We decided to visit Holland for three months when my residency was up in February 1949. Mother financed the trip, since we did not have $1200 to spend on two shipboard tickets.

We left from New York, after riding the Pacemaker train from Chicago to New York City. It was an overnight trip, and we enjoyed the Hudson River Valley scenery in the early morning. We stayed in New York long enough to visit my friends Gerda and Ernest Rudinger, who lived on Long Island. I had been best man at their wedding just before I came to the U.S.

Then we boarded the Veendam (Holland America Line) and began the leisurely 10-day voyage to Holland. The ship was not large, carrying perhaps 250 people. The weather being wintry, we didn't spend a lot of time on deck, but the salon and cabins were comfortable, and there was a library. When we finally docked at Southampton, England, it was in bone-chilling fog. Whether it was the weather, bad food, or sea sickness, 75% of the passengers (including M.J.) were ill crossing the English Channel. As usual, I was lucky and was not sick.

So it was a rather pale and tired bride that met my family! They still are amused to remember that about 10:00 p.m. that first night I looked at her and said, "You'd better get to bed." They interpreted this as my being the authoritative husband and her being the submissive wife, while to her it was an immense relief, an excuse to rest after a very trying day!

So began what was to be for her a seven-month stay with her in-laws. M.J. and I went many places between March and May, notably the tulip fields in early May. It was cold in Holland as usual, since it is rarely hot even in summer. We drove to Belgium for a reunion with my aunt, my mother's sister, and her family.

As my relatives wanted to celebrate our wedding, we enjoyed a wonderful six-course dinner complete with speeches, a custom which was already beginning to disappear in Europe. The next day M.J. and I drove to Luxembourg, a place which was charmingly picturesque.

When we arrived in a little town called Wiltz, where Mary Jean's father had been stationed in 1919 after World War I, we went to the parish priest, who found the Schlottert family for us. Her father had become good friends with this family. The younger family members whom her father had known were married and gone, but the aunt and uncle remembered "Lt. Kennedy," and toasted us with Moselle wine! We also visited the American cemetery in the Ardennes forest, Belgium, where Patton is buried. We saw Bastogne, where General McAuliffe said "Nuts!" to the Germans. It was still pockmarked with bullets.

After this we returned to the Netherlands. I remember well the many dinners in Rotterdam with Mother and the family. They were simple meals much like those in the U. S. It was only 1949, and fuel was still rationed in Holland, so the bedrooms and baths were unheated and only fireplaces in the dining room and living room were lit. The family provided a warmth for both of us, something I am forever grateful for. It would not have been surprising if they had resented me marrying an American.

While we were in Holland, I had been corresponding with Dr. Halloran in Jackson, Minnesota. Dr. Halloran had been in college with M.J.'s father — and with others who could help me in practicing medicine in Minnesota.

I had run into roadblocks in being able to practice in Illinois, and decided to try Minnesota. M.J. and I discussed whether it might be better for her to stay in Holland for the summer while I found us a place to stay and got our things moved. It was the most practical and economical way to do it.

So I took the Nieuw Amsterdam, then the largest ship in the Holland America Line fleet, on May 31st for New York. I had an uneventful trip to New York, unlike the first trip in January 1946 which had taken 18 days because of severe storms.

After I landed, I took the Pacemaker to Chicago. This train was all coach — one had to sit up all night. After arriving in Chicago, I began to get the things packed to ship to Minneapolis.

By this time Dr. Halloran had arranged for me to take the Minnesota Basic Sciences Examination so that I could qualify for a license to practice medicine in that state. After I took it, Dr. Halloran informed me that I had scored among the highest three or four who had ever taken the test. I must admit I was pleased! After that I arranged for a residency in psychiatry at Minneapolis General Hospital.

Having never packed household goods, I was somewhat at a loss and left everything but personal belongings to the movers. We had very little to move except kitchen utensils, plates and bath towels, etc.

From Minneapolis General, where I started in August, I began searching for an apartment. M.J. left Holland on September 25 and arrived in New York October 1st. She took the train to Chicago and another to Minneapolis, where her mother met her with me. Mr. and Mrs. Kennedy had bought a retirement home in the hills of Arkansas, so Mrs. Kennedy came up to greet me while Mr. Kennedy held the fort.

Just as she came, I had found out that the mother-in-law of M.J.'s cousin had a second floor apartment being vacated, so we had an unfurnished place to live for $40 a month. We had to share the bath with Mrs. Foran, our landlady. From the viewpoint of years later it was very simple, but we were delighted, especially with the cost. That, plus food and transportation, left us money at the end of the month on a $100 monthly salary! I remember we went to movies quite often in those days!

So went our days in the second and third year of marriage. I remember that once the hospital put on an entertainment night, and because I was adept at sleight-of-hand — I had practiced a lot in my youth, it was a hobby I delighted in — I was part of the show. The main song, which the whole cast loved and sang with gusto, was "Put another nickel in, in the nickelodeon. All I want is loving you and music, music, music!" I had a lot of fun, and the attention of all the pretty nurses wasn't bad either!

❧ 31 ❧

In 1950, when I finished the General Hospital residency, I arranged to go on the staff of Anoka State Hospital, which was not far from north Minneapolis, an easy drive from where we lived.

A momentous event occurred on January 15th, 1951, when I became a citizen in a memorable ceremony. I will never forget that day, something I had looked forward to all my youth.

Then it began to snow almost incessantly. For six or seven weekends it snowed at least ten inches. Both of us dug the snow out of Mrs. Foran's long driveway so I could get the car out. Finally we gave up. There was a bus to Anoka which stopped at the corner, so I took it until the snow melted enough to get the car out. It was a record snow up until very recently.

In the spring of 1951 we realized that we were soon going to need larger quarters — our first child was on the way. It was sad leaving Mrs. Foran, who had been good to us, but we would need our own bathroom with a baby to take care of. The one bedroom apartment we found was in a suburb of Minneapolis, St. Louis Park. It was farther from Anoka but still accessible by four lane roads. We moved there in June 1951, but it was not for long. The Korean War had been going on for a year, and there was a well-publicized doctor shortage in the armed forces. More and more I worried that if I got settled in practice, I might be drafted, so I decided to volunteer. I was surprised when the Army offered me the option of one, two, or three years, so naturally I took one. I was to report for duty October 15 with the rank of Captain. Our child was due October 8, which did not provide much leeway. We decided that I would drive out to California and report to Camp Cooke, near Santa Maria (this army base no longer exists) while Mary Jean stayed in the apartment until I found quarters for us.

By this time we had some more furniture but had also borrowed some, so most of the belongings would be personal, plus everything for the baby.

In September the baby surprised us by arriving two weeks earlier than expected — a boy, which thrilled his father. Mary Jean's cousin Terry, a nurse at the hospital, laughed when she saw me so excited.

On October 7 the baby was baptized Michael Conrad, with my in-laws and assorted relatives present. Mother was godmother by proxy, and my father-in-law was godfather. It was hard for me to leave with my new little son so fascinating to watch, but I took off in the new Ford which we had bought that year.

I was lucky not to hit snow in the mountains on the way out and arrived safely at Camp Cooke. There I quickly fitted into the Army medical staff. Upon my discharge in 1952 my commanding officer was kind enough to say that I was an excellent diagnostician, and expressed regret at losing me to civilian life.

In the next three months M.J. stayed in Minneapolis tending the baby with the help of her relatives and also her parents, who had come for the baby's baptism and stayed with her about six weeks. I was very glad to have them stay with her as long as I could not be there to help tend the new baby. Meantime I found an apartment in a cottage in a six unit complex with two bedrooms.

Mary Jean got a moving company to pack our things, and she made a reservation on the Southern Pacific for Christmas Day, 1951, there being no reservations left before that.

Her uncle and aunt took her to the train and gave her, the baby, and much baggage (mostly baby stuff) to the porter for safekeeping. She had a bedroom, which was very comfortable, and warmed the baby's feeding bottle in the little sink. The porter kindly offered to baby-sit so that she was able to go to the diner for at least one meal per day, which was a nice change.

The trip was fun, scenic and really no trouble at all. But it was wonderful to see her get off the train as I waited on the platform in Los Angeles. It was a very happy reunion.

❧ 32 ❧

We drove out of L.A. on Route #101 toward Lompoc, which is situated about half way between L.A. and San Francisco, some 5 miles off the coast. The apartment was clean and new, with a modern kitchen and heat in the living room (a wall heater) and bath (the same). To keep the bedrooms warm, we had to leave doors open.

We were soon in a routine. I was at Camp Cooke three nights weekly, so M.J. held the fort with Michael. As a fairly new bride she acknowledged that she had much to learn about housekeeping/baby care, and frequently the housekeeping suffered badly. The sink would be full of dishes and the dust and sticky grime from baby hands would accumulate while she washed diapers in a small washer, rinsed them by hand and then hung them on a portable rack in our tiny back yard. Gradually things got better, and life became more routine!

One night in 1952 we were awakened at about 4:00 a.m. by a loud, continuous noise and the house shaking. It did not occur to us for a minute that we were experiencing an earthquake — when we did, we both jumped out of bed and I grabbed Mike from his crib. We stood in the front door frame, as we had heard this was the safest place in a house. The shaking progressed to a feeling of being on water with waves rippling the surface, and soon subsided. Later we heard that there had been a severe quake (7.8 on the Richter scale) at Tehachapi, 150 miles east of us. This is one of the earthquakes always mentioned in articles about California "temblors," as they are called. It was a scary 10 minutes, and I have no desire to repeat the experience.

❧ 33 ❧

My year with the Army was up in September 1952, since allowance was made for time off, and so forth. We planned to drive back the southern route, since my mother-in-law was visiting us and planned to return to Arkansas. We drove down to L.A. and proceeded across the Mojave Desert at night to avoid the heat of the sun. Practically no car had A/C then, and ours certainly didn't.

With Michael in the back seat on a baby mattress and we three adults in the front — even the 1950 Ford was pretty roomy for three — we took off through Arizona, saw the Grand Canyon in all its majesty, saw Meteor Crater and the Painted Desert, finally leaving Mrs. Kennedy in Albuquerque, where she took the bus back to Arkansas. Then the three of us turned northeast through Kansas toward Rochester, Minnesota where I had arranged to go on the staff of the Rochester State Hospital as its education director.

We settled into the State Hospital compound in October 1952. There were eight houses on the property owned by the state of Minnesota, and we were assigned a very nice three bedroom house there. The staff and wives were very kind and welcoming, and we were soon in a routine which was to last for eight pleasant years during which time our second child, Suzanne Mary, was born in 1956.

My confreres at the State Hospital were Dr. Peterson, chief of staff, and Dr. Jorge Lazarte, who became a close friend, and who lived across the street from us in the compound. The State Hospital offered a chance for experience in helping patients, but I soon learned that what I could do for them was not adequate. I figured with the number of doctors and the number of patients, I could see each one about five minutes a month. There had to be something better than that!

When we came to Rochester, Michael was a baby of thirteen months. It was September 1952 and we had a lovely three bedroom house and friendly neighbors. Soon we had a shaded sandbox for Michael and were settling into a routine. Mike was the center of both our lives, for we had waited three years for his birth, M.J. having lost two early pregnancies before he came along. He was a sweet little boy and lively. As he grew older, I helped him in his play, one winter building a snow fort for the children to play in, and helping him learn how to skate on a little rink I made in the yard.

Mike's best friend in those young years was Ronnie Braun, son of another of the psychiatrists who lived in the compound. Until both of them went to different schools — Mike to the parish school at St. Francis Church, Ronnie to the nearest public school — they played together.

The beginning of school was very important and memorable, both for Mike and for his doting parents. Mary Jean worried a lot that he would be upset about being away from home, so we decided that I would take him into the kindergarten class and introduce him to his teacher. Somewhat to my chagrin, Mike calmly said good-bye to Daddy and walked in without a backward glance. It was as if he had been waiting for this day for a long time. It could have been because of my studious effort to remain calm! It seemed to work!

Our life was really full when Sue was born. When she was little, we called her Suzy, but when she was older she asked us to call her Sue, and that she is called now. Her best friend was Mary Dahlberg, daughter of the Protestant chaplain at the State Hospital. Mary lived just across the street in the compound. Sue was the child most like me in both temperament and looks. I understood her very well.

Life seemed ideal in those years from 1952 to 1960, but as the years wore on, I found that the time I could give to each patient was still far too little. In addition, the psychoanalytic method which I had been taught in medical school did not seem to help many of those with whom I dealt. By the late 1950's I was seriously considering abandoning the specialty of psychiatry for general medicine, but fate intervened.

On one of my visits to Holland to visit my family, I related to my cousin Dick Schretlen, a Benedictine priest, my frustration over the practice of psychiatry. Father Dick asked me if I had ever read the work of a Dutch woman psychiatrist on the relevance of Thomistic rational psychology to neurosis and its treatment. I thought: a woman? and brushed off the information. (I was a true male chauvinist at the time!) I was persuaded, though, to buy one of her books, and thrust it into my suitcase, to be forgotten for months.

One day I had some time on my hands and decided to read Dr. Anna Terruwe's book. I remember how electrified I was. "Why," I told Mary Jean, with much excitement in my voice, "this is the answer! I have been so discouraged about psychiatry, but this — this is the truth! I must get in touch with Dr. Terruwe at once!" And I went off to write her a letter.[1]

I eventually made arrangements to go to visit Dr. Terruwe, ask her many questions and begin to translate two of her books, which appeared in English as *Psychopathic Personality and Neurosis* and *The Neurosis in the Light of Rational Psychology*. I was assisted in the editing by Father Jordan Aumann, O.P., to whom I will always be grateful.

I continued to go to Holland every two years or so, discovering more and more of her unique approach, including a new one on what eventually came to be called in English deprivation neurosis. Dr. Terruwe tells of her discovery: "After several months of psychotherapy had gone by without any noticeable sign of progress (this patient) remarked one day, 'Doctor, nothing that you say has any effect on me. For six months I have been sitting here hoping you would take me to your heart... you have been blind to my needs.'"[2]

---

[1] In 1984, when I visited Dr. Terruwe with Mike and Sue, Dr. Terruwe remembered that letter. "He said he wanted to translate my book, and I thought, 'Who are you?'" She smiled. — Mary Jean.

[2] *Loving and Curing the Neurotic*, p. 124.

❧ *34* ❧

When I discovered Dr. Terruwe's ideas, I became more and more restless and frustrated in the State Hospital job. I began to think of starting a private practice in psychiatry.

My ideas were given a push by the State of Minnesota, which decided to run the state hospitals more directly, including among other things, telling the physicians what to prescribe as medication for the patients. In 1959 the three top physicians at Rochester State Hospital decided to leave. This we did in 1960, but Mary Jean and I had already by that time bought land in order to build a house with attached office. Construction was started in December 1959, and after much travail, which most people experience in building a house, we finally moved in July 1, 1960. Mary Jean was a month away from the birth of our third child, Mike and Sue were feeling the uprooting, and we lived in the house for several weeks while the interior was being finished! In due time, in August, Eleanor Constance was born. Being the baby of the family, she got the direction of both parents and her big brother and sister, including teasing from the latter two.

As time wore on and the older children were away at school, Ellie, as we called her, played card games and cribbage with me. Ellie had a calm temperament that seemed to take everything as it came, and she and I were good friends.

Interestingly enough, all three of the children ended up graduating from the University of Dallas, in Irving, a suburb of Dallas. We had searched for a good Catholic college in the late 1960's and decided to investigate UD. All three of us liked it and its solid Catholicity after visiting it in the summer of 1969. So Mike spent four years there; Sue, after trying elsewhere, also ended up graduating from UD and going on to get an M.A. in politics and literature. Then Ellie decided that she wanted to attend UD also.

But all this was ahead of us in 1960. In September of that year Michael began 4th grade at a new school, St. John's, and we gave an open house to announce my practice. My office consulting room I furnished as much like a comfortable living room as I could, with warm woods and oriental rug hangings and easy chairs. I sat with my patients rather than behind the desk. I fixed up our record player to pipe in music to the waiting room, so no voices could be overheard — even though all the walls had sound deadening material in them. Our dining room was next to the office, and provided a buffer zone of quiet so the house noises did not penetrate.

Oh, how we waited for those first phone calls asking for appointments! I had contacted the clergy and religious of the diocese that I was now in practice, and it just seemed at the time that it took forever. Actually within months my practice was full and there was a waiting list of patients.

My main interest was in the cleric or religious patient, who had such a ripple effect on so many others. From the beginning I saw Dr. Terruwe's ideas succeed as I put them to the test. Where before it was unusual to cure someone, now it became unusual not to cure the patients.

My dedication to St. Thomas' psychology became fervent, and I began to think of myself and Dr. Terruwe writing a book for the American market, incorporating the other books and adding my many case histories to hers. Publicity should persuade many psychiatrists to begin to treat patients with the new ideas about repression and deprivation neurosis.

By the late 1960's the book was finished, but the difficulty of finding an interested publisher who would reach the medical and psychiatric field then became apparent. None would accept the manuscript.

Finally I sent the manuscript to Neil McCaffrey of Arlington House and the Conservative Book Club. The connection was

Mary Jean's cousin Eleanor Kennedy, who had worked for McCaffrey from 1965 to 1968. I am forever grateful for the result. The Conservative Book Club accepted the manuscript, and it was published in 1972, under the title of *Loving and Curing the Neurotic*. Unfortunately, it had a limited appeal for that audience, and publication ceased in a couple of years, after about 5,000 copies had been sold.

❧ 35 ❧

Meanwhile I had a dream, now that my private practice was so successful, to open some kind of residential center for patients, perhaps by building on our property which encompassed 10 acres. But before I began turning this dream into reality, I met a priest psychologist and a nun psychiatrist on the east coast, while I was lecturing in the area of Worcester, Massachusetts.

The two religious professionals seemed very taken with the idea of a residential center for priests and religious. There were many people in that area who were interested, and after much maneuvering, praying and asking for donations, the center became a reality in October 1973, with a formal opening in June 1974 which was attended by Dr. Terruwe and Cardinal Bernard Alfrink of the Netherlands. The center was called the House of Affirmation. All this, of course, entailed the closing of my practice in Rochester, the selling of our home of thirteen years, and the uprooting of the children except for Mike, who had been away at the University of Dallas since 1969. Sue had to leave before her senior year of high school and Ellie before her seventh grade year.

It was a great sacrifice, but as I told the children one night at the dinner table: "I want to do something for the Church before I die." I had a premonition even in youth that I would not live to old age. My father had had a congenital high blood pressure condition, which I had inherited — by 35 I was taking medication for it, and my heart had been affected by what I experienced at Buchenwald. It was time to help the Church — now. So one day in July 1973, we drove away from the home we loved and toward the east, to a hopeful but unknown future.

I prayed hard about all this and was helped by a religious

sister who often had visions. The Lord had indicated to her that we should go, and she presented to me a crucifix which had bled — the sign she had prayed about. With hindsight I see that there was also suffering entailed for me and the family — emotional suffering this time.

For as soon as the new staff began to work together, I began to see there were big problems. The others did not understand the vision of Dr. Terruwe and did not approach treatment the same way.

So after one and a half years I left, citing personal and professional reasons. It was a heart wrenching decision, a profound disappointment.

We had a very large house in the same town as the House of Affirmation. The house had eight bedrooms and three floors, and so when I asked Ellie and Mary Jean (Sue was away at college, and Mike was by then living and working in Dallas) what they would think about taking in four of my patients from the House of Affirmation, they were quite willing to try it. What would I have done without them? These patients did not want to change therapists, so they all moved in, to be housed on the third floor where each had a private room; there was also a big recreation room on that floor. One sister stayed on the second floor, where there were five bedrooms.

This began in February 1975, and the last patient left in August 1976. They stayed for varying times. They saw me for therapy in the big living room where thick double doors could be closed. The family usually only saw them at mealtimes, as they each had instructions not to interfere with our daily lives, and also were to practice what they had learned in therapy. Much of their time was relaxed and free.

We all got along well and the family grew to like the four very much. There were two nuns and two priests, and the four ranged in age from 34 to 65. There were some very amusing, and irritating, times such as when one came down at night to eat, because he was on a medication which made him very hungry.

He made cream of wheat which somehow exploded, hitting the ceiling and walls! He desperately cleaned up and did a good job, for Mary Jean never knew the extent of the problem when she came into the kitchen the next morning!

Another time my mother-in-law stayed with them while we went on vacation. The security system malfunctioned and one of the priests sneaked quietly down the stairs with a baseball bat, the others close behind. They said later they didn't know what they would have done had someone been there!

Over the one and a half years there were many laughs, friendly conversation, and letting our guests just be themselves, as well as therapy from me. It worked very well. All were much improved when they left us. It seems as if a relaxed family atmosphere is very therapeutic.

❧ 36 ❦

I also had a wider practice for the years we remained in Whitinsville after leaving the House of Affirmation, but we now had to think about leaving and settling somewhere else. There were financial angles as well as where a good psychiatric practice could be started.

I favored states without an income tax, so I checked Florida, California, Nevada, and Texas. Nevada seemed good until we found the real estate highly inflated: $150,000 for a three bedroom house, very high for that year (1975). Florida had a great many physicians and California did not appeal either, so Texas became the state we investigated. San Antonio, being very Catholic, appealed to me the most, and we eventually settled there. It would be a nice city in which to retire in about ten years.

On the first of September 1976, having sold the Whitinsville house, we took off for Texas. Mary Jean and I had flown to San Antonio in July to look for a place, to no avail, so when we arrived in San Antonio with Sue and Ellie on September 8th, we took an apartment to stay in while searching for a house. Sue and Ellie were still home, so we all went along for the next three weeks looking for just the right house.

Finally we found one which would take a minimum of fixing up — it had a separate room off the garage which could be an office, so in we moved with rented furniture until the painting and carpentry were finished. By February 1977 my practice was in full swing, booked several weeks in advance. Texans proved friendly and helpful, and we were charmed by the Spanish aura of San Antonio.

Our first contact was with the Right-to-Life office in town. I

214

had been a member of Minnesota Citizens Concerned For Life, and we had known them to be the finest people of our acquaintance in Minnesota. They told us to contact the Catholic Chancery to get hold of Father Tom Collins. I still laugh when I remember the response of the operator at the Chancery: "Oh, you want the abortion priest!"

Our life was soon in a pleasant routine, once the necessary repairs and remodeling were made to make a suitable office out of the game room. That could be a book in itself!

I soon became acquainted with several of the religious superiors in the area, who were very interested in establishing a residential center like the House of Affirmation. But because of my painful experience with HOA, I suggested they wait for some time and give thought to the ideas before acting on them. There has to my knowledge been no further action about this.

Many requests came to me for speaking engagements, and each year I went to Guelph, Ontario to give a seminar with Father Jim Wyse, S.J., Father Remy Limoges, S.J. and Sister Gertrude Wemhoff, O.S.B. In 1980 I was a speaker at the San Diego Charismatic Conference in August, while in May of that year I received the Christian Culture Award from Assumption College, Windsor, Ontario, through the interest of the late Father Stanley Murphy, C.S.B. Receiving this award put me in a group which included Sigrid Undset and Malcolm Muggeridge. I am very proud to be in such company.

≫ 37 ≪

So even though my dream of establishing a residential center for patients was not realized, I came to terms with what God wanted for my life and left the future to His wisdom.

I travelled to Holland in 1979, where I had a good visit with my sisters and brothers and spent some time with Dr. Terruwe. This was during the time Pope John Paul II was in the United States, and Dr. Terruwe and I watched with interest from Holland, while the family was glued to our set in San Antonio!

I had a heart spell in Holland, and spent a day or so in a Nymegen hospital for observation.

Shortly after I returned from Holland, Mary Jean and I went to Mexico on an Oblate mission tour, and again I had heart problems — rapid heart beat — necessitating more medication due to the 7,500 foot altitude in Mexico City. Acapulco proved fine and we enjoyed the days there in lazy fashion on the beach or wandering through the shops.

We arrived home on November 4 to the terrible news of the hostages taken in Iran. Then early in 1980 I fainted at a Serra Club luncheon. My heart was deteriorating, causing a brief cardiac arrest. I was awake on my own in 30 seconds and needed no medical help.

While in Whitinsville I decided to write a book on deprivation neurosis which could be easily understood by laymen. One of the sister patients was an accomplished typist and did the manuscript. I remember discussing with Mary Jean the practical side of writing — the message would be there if I should die, and it also would bring her income.

For a long time I thought about a title — a tentative one was *I Was Never Born* — but I thought it might confuse readers, who might think it referred to abortion. Finally a title came which delighted me and expressed exactly what I wanted to convey: *Born Only Once.* This referred to the fact that each person must have a psychic birth in addition to his physical and spiritual (baptismal) birth. Psychic birth comes with the acceptance of the child for himself by what psychology would call "significant others" — primarily parents.

At the same time I was thinking of making therapy tapes for the many people who might not find it possible to come to me. I did this in the quiet of the night in the big living room with my own taping and microphone equipment. Not being a professional at this, I did a lot of patient experimenting before I got what turned out to be an excellent finished product. At least one thousand sets have gone out over the years.

As the practice settled in, I began to think of rewriting and revising *Loving and Curing the Neurotic,* now out of print 5 years or so. Arlington House suggested I try paperbacks, and I contacted several publishers, finally settling on Alba House through Fr. Anthony Chenevey, its editor. I decided to break *Loving and Curing the Neurotic* into two paperbacks, the first to fully explain deprivation neurosis, the second repression and Dr. Terruwe's unique explanation of it. The former became *Healing the Unaffirmed,* the latter *Psychic Wholeness and Healing.*

In between I decided to write for laymen a kind of handbook in question and answer format, which I titled *Feeling and Healing Your Emotions.* This I wanted to reach Protestants as well as Catholics, so published it through Logos International.

❧ 38 ❦

(Written by Mary Jean)

I am writing the rest of his story, as Koert got busier and busier with writing and giving talks, and had little or no time to write this part of his life.

The five years we lived in San Antonio before Koert's death were very happy ones for the whole family. Koert found camaraderie in his tennis buddies. Tennis players can always find someone to play with — usually several! The courts were directly across the street. He planted a vegetable garden — in Texas there is a spring and fall crop — so we had lots of tomatoes, cucumbers, beans, eggplant, lettuce, green peppers, etc. Koert puttered around the house, fixing things that needed to be fixed.

As for his patients, he found time to write in longhand to out-of-town current and former patients, many of whom wrote to tell me this after his death. With all of this plus his lecturing engagements, full patient schedule, and writing, he never seemed hurried — he led a balanced life, following his own instructions for healthy and happy living. He published through Alba House the two paperback books containing the material in *Loving and Curing the Neurotic*, as *Healing the Unaffirmed* (1976) and *Psychic Wholeness and Healing* (1981). The first was about deprivation neurosis, the second about repression, with an introduction explaining the psychology of the normal individual, an invaluable lesson in Thomistic psychology.

In November 1980, Koert flew to Canada to fulfill a lecture

An Autobiography

engagement at the Hotel Dieu in Kingston, Ontario. The "Hotel" was a hospital, and it was while he was lecturing to a largely medical audience and right across the hall from the emergency room that he suddenly lost consciousness and collapsed, striking the back of his head on a blackboard nearby.

The cardiac team sprang into action and within 60 seconds they had his heart beating again. He had suffered a cardiac arrest. About an hour later, after he was out of emergency and in intensive care, the priest in charge of the seminary, Fr. Brian McNally, called me to tell me what had happened.

By that time Koert was stabilized and eight stitches had been taken in his scalp. He would have to stay two or three days in intensive care. Later that same day Koert called me himself and I remember trying to lighten the situation by saying, "What the hell is going on up there?"

He chuckled and I heard his voice relax. He told me that he remembered nothing — he had not even had any warning — and suddenly found himself waking up in intensive care. To call me, he had persuaded the nurse to wheel his bed out in the hall to a telephone! Later I discovered that Koert had described the incident to a patient in this manner: "It would have been an easy death... just lights out."

After two days his friend Fr. Remy Limoges drove him to Ottawa, where he could take the plane to Dallas. There Mike, Sue and Ellie met him, and Ellie accompanied him back to San Antonio. We were all in a daze. It simply could not have happened to Koert! I suppose the suddenness and import of what had occurred had left us all numb.

Koert insisted on seeing the patients who were scheduled, but two days later he did go with me to see Dr. Block, his cardiologist. We first had lunch with Charles Stiles, a tennis friend and Koert's stockbroker. I think now that Koert wanted me to know Charlie in case anything happened to him. It was a fortunate thing, as Charlie later proved a tremendous help in managing the securities for me.

When we went to see Dr. Block, Koert went in to see him alone and came out after awhile to invite me to come in and ask questions. The only one I could think of to ask was, "What do I do if this happens at home?" to which Dr. Block replied, "You pound as hard on his chest as you can and call EMS."

I remember thinking I would be quite inadequate to do that, not having enough muscle. It was all so unreal and unbelievable, even though intellectually I knew it could happen anytime, suddenly. Emotionally, as I found later, I was utterly unprepared.

❧*39*❦

As time went on, life settled into the usual routine. Koert had scheduled patients as usual, although he was forbidden to travel, and life was calm. He planted his garden in the spring, using the tiller, which necessitated much strenuous effort.

Often while he was out in the yard, I thought to myself, "I am not going to nag him. Life is too short to be forbidden everything he likes to do — if he dies doing this, at least he has been happy doing it." An exam later showed his heart did enlarge again, after having gone down in size for several months.

In the summer of 1981 Koert announced he was going up to the Mayo Clinic, to see if they could do more for him than Dr. Block was able to accomplish. Also during the summer he began to have some gallbladder problems, colic after eating dinner.

In August he flew to Rochester and stayed at a hotel near the Clinic. I learned later of how exhausted the tests made him, but at the time he kept this from me so as not to worry me. He did manage to have several meals at Michael's restaurant, the best eating establishment in the area. After his death, a friend of ours who took him to the airport when he was finished at the Clinic, told me that he seemed preoccupied, and she knew somehow that she would not see him again. Also after his death a patient, who was a nurse, told me he had confided to her that the doctors had found an aneurysm on his heart — he must have known, being a physician, that all the signs pointed to an early death. However, when he returned home and I asked him how he was and what the results were, he said, "Oh, fine," in a way that I knew he wouldn't tell me what they had really said.

In September Fr. Edwin Garvey asked Koert to go to Houston to speak at the University of St. Thomas. It was to be his last trip.

On October 1-4 the National Catholic Physicians Guild was having its annual meeting in San Antonio and he was asked to be the opening night's dinner speaker. He had gotten noticeably thinner, and there were hollows in his cheeks. To me he spoke lightly of his discovery that public speakers were particularly subject to cardiac arrest, but luckily he would be in the midst of his colleagues with the Nix Hospital right across the street. Koert's talk to the Physicians Guild was a really moving one on affirmation — addressed to these doctors for their families and patients. You could have heard a pin drop — and this was an after-dinner speech. It was a great success.

At our home we had a fine get-together the next night with Fr. Charles Corcoran, O.P., Dr. Herbert Ratner, Dr. Hank Kankowski, and Dr. and Mrs. Bernie Klamecki. Fr. Corcoran and Dr. Ratner vied with each other telling jokes — I don't remember a more relaxed and enjoyable evening.

About October 6, Koert told me he was running a fever and did not know what was causing it. All that week he had a normal schedule of patients — by now three days a week, slowly readying for retirement from active practice. There was so much to write! He had mentioned a book on abortion, which he said he could not seem to get around to beginning.

The following Sunday I awoke at 8:00 a.m. to find him sitting in the living room, in considerable pain. His gallbladder was acting up, and he did not go to Mass that morning. Later on that day he seemed better and ate dinner as usual. Monday he had off and was out on several errands. By 10:00 p.m. he was in such pain that he asked me to go to Revco on IH-10 — a 24-hour pharmacy — for some Demerol. I remember thinking the pain must be great for him to ask me to go out at night, which I usually avoided doing. He looked up the dosage in his medical book and went to bed. About 2:00 a.m. he was up again and took another 50 mg. — 150 mg. in all. After that he fell asleep.

Tuesday morning he had patients, and was still in pain. One patient told me later that the pain was so bad he was in tears. She urged him to call his doctor (the patient was an RN) but he managed to get through the time, came in and ate lunch, and saw a 1:00 p.m. patient. Meantime he had called Dr. Block, who told him to meet him at the Nix Hospital. At 2:00 p.m. he packed a small bag and we drove to the Nix. He let me drive, and to me that indicated he was really ill! I thought, "Will he return home again?" But it was a rhetorical question unrelated to the reality of death.

The hospital was very slow in its admitting procedures. Koert was too much in pain to say anything and I was impatient to get him as comfortable as possible in a bed. Finally he was put in a private room and we settled in to wait for the doctor. Koert dozed off while I said the rosary — the Sorrowful Mysteries.

Later Dr. Block and Dr. Brad Oxford, a surgeon and Mayo graduate, and personal friend and surgeon for Dr. Block himself, came in and asked Koert some questions about the pain. Dr. Block assured Koert another of his patients had come through gallbladder surgery and had died of an unrelated disease years later. They decided to wait a day, if possible, for Koert to get the anticoagulants, which would be a risk in surgery, out of his system. Of course, they said, things could change rapidly. After Dr. Block ordered a shot of painkiller, Koert felt much better and was able to eat soft and liquid foods. At 6:30 p.m. I had to leave, as the downtown was no place for a woman driving alone after dark. I told him I wished I could do something for him, but was afraid to touch him as it might cause pain. He looked so sweetly at me and said, "Will you give me a kiss?" That kiss I will never forget.

I was to bring some of his things in the morning, so at 9:00 a.m. I called to see if he had any more items I should bring. He answered the phone with obvious difficulty, and said to come along after mentioning some other items. I was getting ready to go, when 20 minutes later he called again. The doctors had been in to see him and had decided to operate that morning.

I quickly called St. Luke's Catholic Church to leave word for Father Hennessy to pray for Koert and found a friend on the phone. We talked longer than we should have — I never thought of asking for the Anointing of the Sick at the time, but later, after

Koert's death, Father Hennessy told me that because of the situation Koert was in, having surgery, he did anoint him. I was so thankful and immensely grateful to Father for that. I think my dread of what was to come made me refuse to face the reality of death. By the time my mother and I reached his room at the Nix, he had been taken to surgery only minutes before.

We sat in the solarium near the intensive care unit. It was about 11:00 a.m. when we arrived there. It was a godsend that my mother was there to bolster me and keep me occupied by chatting. No news was good news, and finally to my great joy and relief he was wheeled out of the elevator. Dr. Oxford was jubilant — he and Dr. Block had fully expected the heart to give trouble, but it had not. But, he said, the next few days would tell.

After he was settled, Koert asked the nurse if I was there, and she came to get me. He was awake and breathing through a 1/2 face oxygen mask, but could speak and after I held his hand, he asked if Grandma was there. She went in to see him too. We stayed until about 3:00 p.m. and then after checking with the nurse that it was safe to leave and he was resting, we went home so that mother could take a needed nap — she was 87 at the time.

When I began to think of the situation, I realized some of the children should be there so mother would not be alone — also they could then take turns being with Koert. I called them and they agreed to take turns: Ellie until Sunday, Mike after that and Sue after Mike. None of us realized the grave condition Koert was in.

The next day, Thursday, Ellie arrived and went downtown to see her father. He was somewhat confused already — the nurses said that often happened to patients in intensive care and on medication. He was too weak to look at his mail which I had brought. He spoke very little, only saying, "I am so exhausted."

Friday I brought more mail, but Koert was still too exhausted to open any of it. With great effort he filled in a prescription blank for a patient who had forgotten to get it from him the week before. Later in the day Ellie went down to see him, taking my place. Both of us noticed his confusion.

Saturday he continued to be confused and restless, saying he had to care for his patients, and trying to leave his bed. He calmed down somewhat when I told him it was Saturday.

In the afternoon when Ellie was there, he grew loud and demanding, and began to go back in time in his mind. I became more uneasy, but with the assurances of the nursing staff that he was quieting down, when I called later, I did not stay overnight. Apparently he was in and out of a coma during the night, and by morning when I called at 7:30 his blood pressure was falling and could not be stabilized.

I went down to the hospital, leaving Ellie to look after my mother, trying not to think what was in store. The nurse in S.I.C.U. told me that they still could not control his blood pressure, and she gave me a hug before going back to her patient.

Why didn't I ask her if I could see Koert? I guess many people don't think to do this, believing the staff will call them if it is possible to see the patient. At 9:45 a.m. I heard the staff calling Dr. Block on the intercom to call S.I.C.U. and sensed that Koert must be dying. I had not been able to pray, but began trying to think of a prayer for the dying. About 10:15 the prayer, "Now Thou dost dismiss Thy servant, O Lord," suddenly came into my mind. I learned later it must have been almost precisely the moment of his death, and I believe it was his last message to me — that it was all right, that he was with God.

About 10:30 Dr. Oxford came out, looking around distractedly. I supposed he had come to call me in to tell me that Koert was dying. I remember asking, "Is it very bad, Doctor?" And he shook his head and said, "He's gone." I was so stunned that all I could say was, "Oh, I was so afraid of that." He comforted me as well as he could. He told me of the emergency measures they had taken to save Koert, all in vain.

Koert's funeral Mass was concelebrated on October 22, 1981 by ten priests who had been good friends. Many others who were close to him attended as well as his sister from the Netherlands. He is buried in Fort Sam Houston National Cemetery.

Epilogue

This is written 12 years after Koert's death. In the interim I have been utterly astounded in the steady interest of the public in his work. When he died, there were many orders on hand for books and tapes, and by the time I began, with the help of the children, to go through the mail, I realized I should go ahead as he had and continue the mail orders. This continues to be a small but steady business. People still write often, mostly from the U.S. but also from countries where English is spoken such as Canada, England, Ireland, Australia, New Zealand, Japan, Hong Kong, Indonesia, Philippines, South Africa, Israel, Kenya, and Ethiopia. Priests have also written from Rome, where they were studying at the Angelicum. It convinces me all the more of the truth of which Koert wrote and spoke. This psychology, based on the truths of Aquinas and *true* modern discoveries, appeals to very basic needs in people. I hope and pray that these ideas can be kept before the public by continued publication of the books. The knowledge is crucially important to building an authentic psychology of and for modern man. The anthropology upon which psychology relies today is certainly *not* that "man is made in God's image," as Pope John Paul II said at Puebla, Mexico to the assembled Mexican bishops. Unless and until we turn back to a God-centered world, we are not likely to produce cures in psychiatry and psychology which bring normalcy, happiness and peace to people. Restoring a person only to functioning is not enough. Koert thought this was all important, and he spent himself letting everyone know who would listen. His life was tremendously worthwhile, because he did everything he could to make the world better.

Requiescat in pace.

Mary Jean Baars
October 31, 1993